Quality Questioning

Research-Based Practice to Engage Every Learner

A Joint Publication

CORWIN PRESS

ÆL

Jackie Acree Walsh

Beth Dankert Sattes

CORWIN PRESS
A Sage Publications Company
Thousand Oaks, California

For information:

Corwin Press
A Sage Publications Company
2455 Teller Road
Thousand Oaks, California 91320
www.corwinpress.com

Sage Publications Ltd.
1 Oliver's Yard
55 City Road
London EC1Y 1SP
United Kingdom

Sage Publications India Pvt. Ltd.
B-42 Panchsheel Enclave
New Delhi 110017 India

Printed in the United States of America

Library of Congress Cataloging-in-Publication Data

Walsh, Jackie A.
    Quality questioning: Research-based practice to engage every learner / Jackie A. Walsh and Beth D. Sattes.
    p. cm.
    Includes bibliographical references and index.
    ISBN 978-1-4129-0985-3 (cloth) – ISBN 978-1-4129-0986-0 (pbk.)
    1. Questioning. 2. Thought and thinking. I. Sattes, Beth D. (Beth Dankert) II. Title. LB1027.44W35 2005
    371.39—dc22   2004014965

This book is printed on acid-free paper.

11 12   10 9

Acquisitions Editor:	Faye Zucker
Editorial Assistants:	Gem Rabanera and Stacy Wagner
Production Editor:	Diane S. Foster
Copy Editor:	Carla Thomas McClure
Typesetter:	Dawn Pauley
Proofreader:	Publication Services and Marilyn Slack
Indexer:	Laurie Winship

Contents

What Have We Learned From Our Work? Improving Questioning Is Not Just for Teachers Anymore

Focus Questions

What discrete behaviors are associated with quality questioning?

Why is it important to teach students the skills of quality questioning?

What is the organization of this book?

In a classroom atmosphere conducive to good questions and questioning, students realize a shared responsibility for their learning.
—Francis Hunkins, *Teaching Thinking Through Effective Questioning*

Over the past decade-and-a-half, we have been working with teachers to improve classroom questioning. We began this work because of a shared belief that quality questions and questioning are at the heart of good teaching and learning. This belief sprang from our respective experiences as classroom teachers—Jackie's as a high school social studies teacher and Beth's from her work in early childhood and special education. Two decades of research on teacher effectiveness—spanning the 1970s and 1980s—validated our independently derived intuitions. And so we began reviewing the research and literature on effective questioning and organizing this robust knowledge base for delivery in workshops and in-service sessions.

Early on, we identified key teacher questioning behaviors associated with increases in student achievement. Our mission was to assist teachers in developing deeper understandings of these research-based connections and to demonstrate associated skills such as the use of wait times, higher-level questions, and so forth. By 1989, we had organized these research-based behaviors into a framework or model that served as the content focus for a long-term professional development process designed to assist teachers in changing deeply ingrained behaviors so that they would align with best practice (see Figure 1, QUILT Framework). We named this professional development process *Questioning and Understanding to Improve Learning and Thinking*, which soon became known by the acronym QUILT. The organization of this book mirrors the QUILT Framework.

Figure 1

QUILT Framework

Stage 1: Prepare the Question
- Identify instructional purpose
- Determine content focus
- Select cognitive level
- Consider wording and syntax

Stage 2: Present the Question
- Indicate response format
- Ask the question
- Select respondent

Stage 3: Prompt Student Responses
- Pause after asking question
- Assist nonrespondent
- Pause following student response

Stage 4: Process Student Responses
- Provide appropriate feedback
- Expand and use correct responses
- Elicit student reactions and questions

Stage 5: Reflect on Questioning Practice
- Analyze the questions
- Map respondent selection
- Evaluate student response patterns
- Examine teacher and student reactions

The original structure for the professional development process incorporated in QUILT reflected current research about effective teacher learning; namely, that it must be long-term and personalized, while incorporating peer coaching and opportunities for teachers to learn together. The focus for change was clearly on the teacher. During the early years of QUILT, however, we learned that while most teachers already **possessed knowledge about** the basics of effective questioning, many were finding it exceedingly **difficult to change behaviors.** From conversations with teachers emerged an aha: teachers, even when collaborating with one another to improve practice, cannot change the dynamics of classroom questioning by themselves. They must teach new behaviors such as Wait Times 1 and 2 to students and, with their students, adopt classroom norms that support these behavior changes. Increasingly, we conceptualized quality questioning as a student-centered, collaborative process—not a teacher-centered, teacher-directed classroom enterprise. This new understanding permeates the first five chapters of this book, and it resulted in the addition of a sixth chapter, which goes beyond our original QUILT Framework. The seventh chapter describes methods and benefits of whole-school adoption of effective questioning practice, and the closing chapter reviews the ideas presented throughout the book.

While we assume that most readers will want to begin with Chapter 1 and read straight through, you may choose to delve into the chapters that most interest you. Keep in mind, however, that classroom questioning is a dynamic, holistic process. Each of the stages in our Framework contains behaviors that depend upon and/or interact with behaviors in other stages. For example, wait times are unnecessary and even silly unless used in conjunction with quality questions. Hence, we recommend that you read the chapters in sequence to gain maximum benefit from the book.

Focus questions, which precede each chapter, forecast objectives for the reader. You may also use these as tools to think back over the contents of each chapter. In turn, each chapter concludes with a set of *questions for reflection.* These may serve as tools for reflection on your own practice or, alternately, as questions to prompt collegial dialogue. Finally, we have included as many practical tools, techniques, and strategies as possible, given the limitations of this type book. Our hope is that you will try some of these new strategies with your students and let us know, by e-mail, of your experience. We welcome your feedback. We also invite you to visit the QUILT home page at www.ael.org/quilt to stay informed of our ongoing work on effective questioning.

We are grateful for the opportunity to write this book, which is an important milestone in our journey to share our passion for classroom questioning as key to quality teaching and learning. We could not have accomplished this, however, without the help and support of many individuals. First, we acknowledge the unyielding support of our colleague Sandra R. Orletksy, associate director of the Regional Educational Laboratory at AEL. Sandra served as director of the QUILT project from its inception and demonstrated her faith in our work in countless ways over the years. Second, we recognize all of the teachers and administrators who have participated in our training sessions and contributed to our expanded understanding of the dynamics of classroom questioning. Many have shared personal stories and resources that we've included herein. Next, we thank all of those who assisted with the preparation of this manuscript. We credit Carla McClure, writer and editor at AEL, for the care, enthusiasm, and high level of competence she brought to the editing of the manuscript. We are also grateful to Dr. Robert Childers for "shepherding" us through the writing phase and to Dawn Pauley for the design and layout of the manuscript. And, we thank Faye Zucker, our editor at Corwin Press, for asking us to write this book and for assisting us during the conceptualization stage. Finally, we acknowledge the understanding and support of our respective families—Jackie's children, Catherine and Will; and Beth's husband, Lyle, and her children, Chris and Michael.

Jackie Acree Walsh, WALSHJA@aol.com
Beth Dankert Sattes, beth@enthusedlearning.com

Acknowledgments

Corwin Press extends its thanks to the following reviewers for their contributions to this book:

Patricia Herr, Ball's Bluff Elementary School, Leesburg, VA

Susan Hudson, School Improvement Services, Nashville, TN

Douglas Llewellyn, St. John Fisher College, Rochester, NY

Teresa Miller, Kansas State University, Manhattan, KS

Kathy O'Neill, Southern Regional Education Board, Atlanta, GA

About the Authors

Jackie Acree Walsh, Ph.D., and **Beth Dankert Sattes** are co-developers of *Questioning and Understanding to Improve Learning and Thinking* (QUILT), a nationally validated professional development program on effective questioning. They are also co-authors of *Inside School Improvement* (2000) and co-presenters of the Video Journal in Education series *Questioning to Stimulate Thinking* (1999). These two former classroom teachers have trained hundreds of administrators and teachers across the nation in effective questioning.

Their other joint ventures have focused on creating effective professional development for educators, sharing leadership for continuous school improvement, and creating a culture for high-performance learning communities. A recent example of their work is the design and delivery of professional development for School Improvement Specialists—consultants or staff who work to develop the capacity of schools to improve achievement for all students. They have also developed professional development modules on improving school culture (for the Southern Regional Education Board) and leading learning communities (for the Alabama Leadership Academy).

Jackie Acree Walsh holds a bachelor's degree in political science from Duke University, a master's degree in teaching (M.A.T.) from the University of North Carolina at Chapel Hill, and a Ph.D. in education administration and supervision from the University of Alabama. Beth Dankert Sattes holds a bachelor's degree in psychology from Vanderbilt University and a master's degree in early childhood special education from Peabody College. Both Jackie and Beth have served as faculty for the National Staff Development Council's Academy. They are senior research and development specialists for AEL, a not-for-profit corporation based in Charleston, West Virginia.

Jackie Acree Walsh

Beth Dankert Sattes

The Corwin Press logo—a raven striding across an open book—represents the union of courage and learning. Corwin Press is committed to improving education for all learners by publishing books and other professional development resources for those serving the field of K-12 education. By providing practical, hands-on materials, Corwin Press continues to carry out the promise of its motto: "Helping Educators Do Their Work Better."

AEL, founded in 1966 as a not-for-profit corporation, provides rigorous research, professional development, and consulting services to clients in the education arena. Services include research design and implementation, comprehensive research reviews, intensive product and program evaluations and field trials, consulting services, and award-winning professional development programs. The name "AEL" originated with the first program the corporation operated—the Appalachia Educational Laboratory—but today's AEL is national in scope and provides a range of services to private and government agencies.

The content of this publication was developed, in part, with funds from the Institute of Education Sciences (IES), U.S. Department of Education, under contract number ED-01-CO-0016. Its contents do not necessarily reflect the views of IES, the Department, or any other agency of the U.S. government. AEL is an equal opportunity/affirmative action employer.

Chapter 1:
How Can Quality Questioning Transform Classrooms? Questioning to Advance Thinking, Learning, and Achievement

Focus Questions

How can effective questioning help transform a traditional, teacher-centered classroom into a student-centered, inquiry-oriented community of learners?

What are the connections between quality questions and student learning and achievement?

Why are there gaps between what we know about effective questioning and what we do in classrooms?

Questioning. Thinking. Understanding. These three processes interact in a dynamic fashion to advance student learning, performance, and achievement. Think of these classroom processes as action verbs that create the energy for student work, the fuel for learning. Can you picture the vitality of the teacher and students in a community of learners committed to questioning, thinking, and active understanding? Consider the following vignette, which embodies one vision for such a classroom. As you read this classroom scenario, imagine you are an observer whose task is to identify the norms, structures, and teacher and student behaviors that make this a student-centered, inquiry-oriented community of learners.

As you enter the classroom of A. Thoughtful Teacher, you immediately feel the energy generated by the students' curiosity and excitement for learning. Seated in groups of four, students are formulating collective responses to a focus question written on the whiteboard. The teacher asks the designated reporters from each group to raise their hands. She calls on one of them, who offers a response.

"Thoughtful" waits after the student stops speaking, then says, "I'd like to get behind the thinking that led you to this response. What reasons did you discuss?" The student elaborates on her initial answer. Thoughtful then asks the entire class if they can accept this answer as a well-reasoned one: "Thumbs up, if you think this is an acceptable response; thumbs down, if you cannot follow the argument."

Thoughtful scans the room, noting that all students have their thumbs up. She then asks if there were any different answers to the question. A student raises his hand, and Thoughtful listens actively to this answer, again probing to find out the reasoning behind the response. When this student completes his explanation, another student poses a question: "I want to know if your group identified examples of this concept at work." This student query prompts a five-minute interchange among students—with students from each small group participating.

Thoughtful asks the students to think back on the ideas they've heard in response to the initial question. She pauses for 10 seconds or so, then asks students to share the ideas they've identified—one at a time. As students speak, Thoughtful creates a concept map, which displays each idea and its relationship to others. She instructs the students to talk for a few minutes in their small groups about what this graphic organizer says to them. "As you talk," says Thoughtful, "identify any lingering questions you may have about this topic. Write each question on a separate Post-it note so that you can report out to the whole class."

Students talk quietly in their groups. As you look around the room, you note that all students seem to be engaged. You also observe that students are actively listening to one another and taking notes from time to time. While the students are discussing, Thoughtful moves around the room and listens in on each group's conversation. She seems to be monitoring each group's activity at all times.

After about five minutes, Thoughtful asks for lingering questions. She moves in round-robin fashion from one group to another, asking the designated reporter in each group to read one of their questions and post it in the designated area in the classroom. "If your group had the same question as a previous group, affirm their question and offer another if you have one." When the students' questions are exhausted, Thoughtful points to the six clusters of related questions and says: "I am really pleased with the thinking behind each of these questions. You are moving your thinking to higher levels. Look. These questions are at the evaluation level. What will we have to do in order to answer these?"

One student raises her hand; Thoughtful waits for another three seconds. Other hands go up. She calls on a student who did not speak in the previous discussion, who says, "We'll have to decide on what basis we'll make our judgments." Thoughtful waits, and the student adds: "You know. We'll need to develop some criteria so that we can determine which of our answers are appropriate."

Thoughtful looks around the room of these seventh graders—making eye contact with each student. She states: "I am pleased at the way each of you have honored our classroom norms today." She points to the norms posted on one of the bulletin boards and continues: "I could tell that you were actively listening to one another because you did a lot of "piggy-backing" on one another's responses—and you questioned one another. This type of listening is really key to our thinking together."

She then asks the students to identify other norms that they honored during the discussion. She writes the students' comments beneath a column on the board headed with a plus sign. "Are there ways we might improve our discussions?" she wonders aloud. "Talk in your small groups about areas in which we may need improvement in our classroom community." Thoughtful asks for group sharing once again and posts these comments beneath a column headed with a minus sign.

Thoughtful looks at the clock and comments: "We have only five minutes of class left. Would you open your journals and make your entry for today—noting how you felt about your own participation in class? What helped you learn today? What got in your way?" As the students reflect and write, Thoughtful moves to the doorway—ready to interact with students as they pass to another class.

Norms Shape the Learning Experience

What norms did you identify that seemed to guide the students and teacher as they went about the business of learning and teaching? Read through the following norms, and think about the extent to which each one is a part of the culture of A. Thoughtful Teacher's classroom.

- We all need time to reflect on past experiences if we are to gain new understandings.
- We all need time to think before speaking.
- We all need time to think out loud and complete our thoughts.
- We learn best when we formulate and answer our own questions.
- We learn from one another when we listen with attention and respect.
- When we share talk time, we demonstrate respect, and we learn from one another.

Did you note the instances in which Thoughtful provided students time to think—both before calling on a student to speak and also after an individual student stopped speaking? Teacher pauses at these two points promote student thoughtfulness, resulting in more complete and correct student answers.

A. Thoughtful Teacher is intentional in making room for student questions—both spontaneous and planned. Also, active and respectful listening—by both students and teacher—seems to be a hallmark of this classroom community.

The teacher encourages students to draw upon their own and their peers' experiences and prior knowledge as they grapple with new concepts and ideas.

If inquiry and individual engagement are to characterize a classroom, then the teacher must proactively work with students to establish norms that support this orientation. For example, a teacher might introduce the norm *We all need time to think before speaking* by sharing research from Mary Budd Rowe (1972) about Wait Time 1 in this manner:

> "Sometimes, when I ask a question, several of you raise your hands right away. You know an answer immediately and you want to share it! Others of you are still thinking. And that's OK. In fact, I'm going to ask all of us to take more time before we speak and to use that time to think. Because even if you have an answer right away, if you think about the question for a little while before you speak, you may come up with another answer or a better answer. Why do you think it would be good to take some time to think before speaking?"

Following some discussion by the students, the teacher might continue:

> "A researcher named Dr. Rowe has actually studied how long we should wait and think—and what happens when we take the time to think after a question is asked. She discovered that if we wait three to five seconds before anyone speaks, student answers are better! The answers are more complete, they are longer, and they are more 'on target' with the question. She also found that students are more sure of their answers. They don't just guess as often."

After students demonstrate an initial understanding of this norm, it can be reinforced through practice and feedback.

> "Let's try this Wait Time 1. I'm going to ask a question, and then I want all of us to say together, 'one-thousand-and-one, one-thousand-and-two, one-thousand-and-three.' Then I'll call on someone to answer. OK?"

> "How do the two major political parties in our country select their presidential candidates?—OK, one-thousand-and-one, one-thousand-and-two, one-thousand-and-three. Carmen."

> "How does it feel to wait that long before being called upon to answer a question?"

> "What might be the value of waiting and thinking before speaking?"

> "Now I want you to practice this in your teams. Team leaders,

you'll find a set of questions in your folders. You are to facilitate a team discussion, using Wait Time 1 after posing each question."

The teacher might circulate around the room, monitoring and making notes for feedback that she can give to the class at the end of the exercise. She could also invite individuals in the small groups to give feedback to their group leaders. Finally, she might debrief the activity with the whole group—probing again to encourage students to reflect on the value of this norm to their learning.

Norms can be defined as stated or unstated group expectations related to individual behavior. They develop formally and informally as people interact with one another; over time, these norms become behavioral blueprints for individuals to follow (Deal & Peterson, 1998). Teachers can use norms to help students become comfortable as active participants in their learning.

Structures "Scaffold" Behaviors

A. Thoughtful Teacher does not leave student participation to chance. She creates structures that engage *all* students in thinking and responding to *all* questions. She organizes students to work in cooperative groups. She considers individual students' strengths and personal qualities as she assigns them to work together in pairs or groups of four. Thoughtful knows that cooperative response strategies are powerful ways to engage all students in thinking, talking, and making meaning of concepts under study. Additionally, she incorporates signaled responses (e.g., thumbs up/thumbs down) and work samples (e.g., use of small dry-erase boards for individual responses)—especially to check for student understanding. Occasionally, she uses the traditional mode of questioning— posing a question and calling on individual students to respond—but this is the exception, not the rule.

Because student use of nonlinguistic representations is associated with achievement gains (Marzano, Pickering, & Pollock, 2001, p. 73), A. Thoughtful Teacher uses devices such as concept maps to help students connect new informa- tion, prior learning, and discrete bits of information. This, in turn, assists students in transferring new learnings to long-term memory.

In this student-centered classroom, students have many opportunities to reflect on their own thinking and learning. Thoughtful provides them with the tools, structures, and time for such reflection. Students reflect as a whole group when asked to what extent they honored classroom norms during discussion. Students also reflect individually through journaling. These planned opportunities for reflection reinforce Thoughtful's belief that this class is about each student's learning and that each student is responsible for his or her own learning.

Student and Teacher Roles and Responsibilities Change

The vision of a classroom as a community of learners challenges traditional views of teaching, learning, and questioning. The conventional model of teaching as "knowledge transmission" treats students as sponges that absorb a teacher's wisdom. In the traditional classroom, knowledge is static, inert, and independent of learners. Learning involves listening to the teacher, reading, and studying in order to recall information on demand. Teachers use classroom questions primarily to evaluate students' ability to remember information.

Thoughtful's classroom contrasts sharply with this traditional model. She views learning as a social activity that requires students to interact with their teacher and peers as they engage with the content. Her view of her role corresponds to the one presented by Wiggins and McTighe (2000, p. 298)—teacher as designer of curricular and instructional activities that facilitate the interactions required for learning to the level of understanding. This view of teacher and student roles acknowledges questioning to be a core function of both learning and teaching (Perkins, 1992; Hunkins, 1995; and Wells, 2001). Inquiry, constructivism, and active learning are compatible with this view of teacher and student roles.

Recent reports issued by professional associations in mathematics, reading, science, social science, writing, and art support this new view of teaching, learning, and questioning. Among the recommendations proposed by these national curriculum reports:

- *Less* whole-class, teacher-directed instruction (e.g., lecturing)
- *Less* student passivity (e.g., sitting, listening, receiving, absorbing information)
- *Less* presentational, one-way transmission of information from teacher to student
- *Less* prizing and rewarding of silence in the classroom
- *Less* classroom time devoted to fill-in-the-blank worksheets, dittos, workbooks, and other "seatwork"
- *Less* student time spent reading textbooks and basal readers
- *Less* attempt by teachers to thinly "cover" large amounts of material in every subject area
- *Less* rote memorization of facts and details (Thompson & Zueli, 1999, pp. 4-5)

Professional organizations recommend more experiential, inductive, hands-on learning; more active learning; more emphasis on higher order thinking;

more responsibility transferred to students for their work; and more cooperative, collaborative activity to develop the classroom as an interdependent community (pp. 5-6).

These recommendations led Charles Thompson and John Zeuli (1999) to the following view of instructional improvement:

> The key questions for reform . . . are whether teachers understand that students must think in order to learn and whether they know how to provoke, stimulate, and support students' thinking. . . . The idea that students must create their own understandings by thinking their way through to satisfactory resolutions of puzzles and contradictions runs counter to conceptions of knowledge as facts, teaching as telling, and learning as memorizing. (p. 349)

These authors argue that we teachers must focus our professional learning upon knowledge, skills, and beliefs that will enable us to move from the traditional classroom in which most of us spent our years as students to the more student-centered, inquiry-oriented classroom embodied in what we call a Quality Questioning classroom (p. 371).

What would such a classroom look like? The chart on page 8 displays a range of teacher and student behaviors associated with a Quality Questioning classroom. Individual reflection and collegial dialogue around the beliefs, behaviors, and results outlined in this chart can serve as a beginning point for the type of transformative learning Thompson and Zeuli suggest. Notice that teachers assume different roles in recitation (where the primary purpose is to check for student understanding of content) than in discussion (where the primary purpose is to facilitate student thinking at the highest cognitive levels). Both types of interaction are valued and addressed. Shared beliefs underpin teacher and student behaviors and inspire classroom norms. The "Results for Students" column summarizes the predictable outcomes for learners in Quality Questioning classrooms.

"Learning is a consequence of thinking."

David Perkins, *Smart Schools: From Training Memories to Educating Minds,* p. 8

Like Stephen Covey, author of *The Seven Habits of Highly Effective People,* we believe it prudent to "begin with the end in mind." The chart offers a graphical depiction of the kind of classroom we envision for readers of this book. Woven throughout each chapter in this book are tools and concepts teachers can use to turn this vision into a reality—for themselves and for their students.

What a Quality Questioning Classroom Looks Like

Shared Beliefs	Behaviors	Student Outcomes
Good questions help students learn. All students can respond to all questions. All students' answers deserve respect. Think time is important. Students will ask questions when confused or curious. All students can think and reason—beyond rote memory. Divergent thinking is important. Not all questions have one right answer.	**Teachers** • Ask clear, focused, and purposeful questions • Ask questions at all cognitive levels • Allow Wait Time 1 after asking • Allow Wait Time 2 after students answer • Give each student an equal chance to answer • Invite and allow time for student questions **During recitations, teachers** • Use a variety of response formats • Give appropriate feedback • Help students answer correctly—rephrase, prompt, and cue when needed • Ensure that correct answers are heard by all **During discussions, teachers** • Probe and redirect • Encourage students to interact with other students **Students** • Pay attention to all questions and answers • Think of answers to all questions • Are on alert to answer all questions aloud • Answer questions at the appropriate cognitive level • Use wait times to think about answers • Give wait time to others when asking questions • Ask questions when confused • Ask questions when curious • Make meaning out of facts	**In the classroom, students** • Know facts • Develop understandings based on facts • Use knowledge to solve problems and make decisions • Develop new products and ideas • Make inferences and draw conclusions • Hypothesize and speculate • Know and use effective questioning skills: —rephrase, cue, probe, and redirect —use Wait Times 1 and 2 —give meaningful feedback —ask questions at different cognitive levels • Thoughtfully answer teacher and peer questions • Ask many high-quality questions

Questions and Questioning Form the Core of Teaching and Learning

As new views of teaching and learning emerge, so does a different way of thinking about questioning. Francis Hunkins (1995) observes

> We are shifting from viewing questions as devices by which one evaluates the specifics of learning to conceptualizing questions as a means of actively processing, thinking about, and using information productively. Many educators are weaning students from believing that questions are phrased to attain certain answers and are helping them to accept questions as key vehicles that elicit awareness of the diversity, complexity, and richness of knowledge. More educators are assisting students in comprehending that questions are linguistic goals that enable thinking and production of knowledge. (p. 4)

The kinds of questions that Hunkins suggests are not those found in a game of Trivial Pursuit, but rather those that lead learners to better understandings of the structure of knowledge and the relevance of this knowledge to their personal lives. Chapter 2 presents tools teachers can use to formulate quality questions that lead students to higher levels of thinking.

If questions are vehicles for thought, then the questioning process determines *who* will go along for the ride. *Teacher questioning behaviors affect which students learn how much.* For example, teachers tend to call on high achievers much more frequently than low achievers, which provides these academically able students with an additional edge. A usual result of this practice is that, over their years of schooling, low achievers become accustomed to low expectations. They tune out and turn off. Most of us can be much more intentional about equalizing response opportunities for all students in our classes. Chapter 3 presents strategies for actively engaging all students in thinking and responding.

Another way teachers influence student learning via questioning is through the use of *wait time.* The tendency to wait (or not) for a student response has been found to vary, depending on whether the respondent is a high achiever or a low achiever. The provision of cues, clues, and other prompts to students who do not immediately respond follow this same pattern. Our usual questioning patterns again favor the high-achieving students, and as a result, they derive much more from questioning episodes than do lower achievers in the same classroom. In Chapter 4, we'll explore ways to prompt students effectively so that they are more fully engaged in thinking and answering.

The questioning process is not only a vehicle for eliciting answers from students. It can also keep them thinking and learning beyond an initial correct response. What teachers do with student responses (e.g., move students to ask their own questions or to extend a peer's response) has a dramatic impact on the extent to which students continue their journey of thinking and learning. Chapter 5 explores the impact of teacher feedback and other teacher moves upon student thinking and talking, while Chapter 6 looks at strategies to develop students as questioners.

Chapters 2-6, then, focus on questioning as the core of teaching and learning, while Chapters 7-8 show how a focus on questioning can enhance the professional learning of teachers. The remainder of Chapter 1 examines the gap between current and best practice in using questions to promote thinking and learning.

Gaps Exist Between Best Practice and Current Practice

You met A. Thoughtful Teacher at the beginning of this chapter. She exemplifies the use of questioning to promote thinking and learning. But "Thoughtful" is not typical of K-12 teachers. Studies conducted for well over 100 years about teachers' use of questioning strategies show that there has been very little change in classroom practice, related to questioning, over all those years.

A. Well-Meaning Teacher: A Look at Current Practice

To summarize current practice across our schools, we invite you to meet A. Well-Meaning Teacher, who believes—as do most of us—that classroom questions are very important to teaching and learning. If you asked Well-Meaning her reasons for asking questions, she would reply:

> "Oh, well, that's easy to answer. I ask questions to find out if my students have completed their assignments and, of course, to let them know what I expect them to learn."

And question she does! In a typical 55-minute class period, Well-Meaning asks an average of 50 questions, and she takes great pride in this.

> "The more questions, the better, I always say! We have a lot of material to cover in this class—and it's my job to cover it all!"

Well-Meaning almost always calls on volunteers to answer her questions—those who raise their hands first and look most eager.

> "I like to reward those who've done their work."

After calling on a student, Well-Meaning waits less than one second for the student to begin answering and then quickly calls on another.

> "We don't have any time to spare. I have to keep things moving fast or I'll lose them. And I certainly wouldn't want to embarrass anyone."

If a student gives an incorrect or incomplete answer, she usually says something like "uh-huh" or "okay" and redirects the question to another student.

"If a student tries to answer, I like to give her some credit for trying, but I can't waste valuable class time drawing her out."

Well-Meaning does not encourage student questions and intentionally avoids calling on certain students who always seem to have questions.

"It's in the best interest of everyone to stay on the subject. After all, we must cover all of the curriculum!"

We Don't Always Do What We Think We're Doing

Teachers seem to know what constitutes "best practice," but we aren't always good monitors of our own performance. In one study, for example (Susskind, 1979), teachers were asked the following questions about the ideal and actual rates of student and teacher questions:

- How many questions do you think you ask in a 30-minute period?
- How many questions would be desirable?
- How many questions do your students ask?
- How many student questions would be ideal?

What would your response be to these questions? In the study, teachers estimated that they asked 15 questions in a 30-minute period; they also thought that 15 questions was the desired rate of teacher question-asking. These same teachers estimated that students in their classes were asking about 10 questions, which was below their desired target of 15.

When these same teachers were observed, the data were very different from the teacher estimates. Teachers asked an average of 50.6 questions; students posed only 1.8 questions.

The teachers were shocked by these findings. In fact, they refused to believe them until they listened to an audiotape of their own classrooms and counted the number of teacher and student questions. This is evidence that we don't always do what we know to be good practice; and we may not even be aware of that!

What would an audiotape of your classroom reveal?

Research About Current Practice and Implications for Change

Look at each of Well-Meaning's practices and see what the corresponding research indicates.

Research Finding #1: Teachers ask many questions.

Well-Meaning asked 50 questions in a class period. It is a consistent and well-documented finding that teachers ask a lot of questions. Research conducted nearly a century ago showed that teachers asked between one and four questions per minute. In a summary of research on questioning published in 1971, Gall concluded that teachers typically ask between one and three questions per minute. In our own study (Appalachia Educational Laboratory, 1994), 95 teachers were asked to videotape themselves in a classroom episode where questioning was the primary instructional strategy; the average number of questions asked in 15 minutes was 43 (two to three questions per minute).

You may remember that Thoughtful posed very few questions. Which is better—only a few questions or many questions? Unfortunately, studies are not available on how the number of questions asked affects student learning. Many educators subscribe to the belief that fewer questions, well formulated and thoughtfully posed, do more to promote student thinking than a barrage of questions. Interestingly, however, it seems that asking questions is better than not asking. In a study of the effectiveness of the recitation strategy, in which teachers pose many low-level and recall questions, Gall and others (1978) found that students who participated in a traditional recitation (after reading a passage of text) learned more than students who were not asked questions about the reading.

Implication: Questions promote student learning. Teachers should plan their questions before asking to ensure that questions match the instructional objectives and promote thinking. A few carefully prepared or selected questions are preferable to large numbers of questions.

Research Finding #2: Most teacher questions are at the lowest cognitive level—known as fact, recall, or knowledge.

It makes sense that if teachers are asking one to three questions per minute, the questions do not require much higher order thinking. How much could students be thinking if they are responding to questions every 20 to 30 seconds? In fact, research confirms that only about 20 percent of the questions posed in most classrooms require thinking at higher levels (Gall, 1984).

The research that links the cognitive level of teacher questions to student achievement is mixed. In their review of studies, Redfield and Rousseau (1981) concluded that the use of higher-level questioning is positively related to improved student achievement. Others have reached the opposite conclusion. Still other researchers have concluded that young students and low-income students—who are learning basic skills—benefit most from low-level questions; whereas middle and high school students appear to have higher achievement when exposed to more higher-level questions (Gall, 1984). Even with the differences in the findings, most researchers conclude that higher-level questions promote the development of thinking skills.

This area certainly needs more study. It is important to consider the context of the studies. It seems likely, in consideration of the nationwide emphasis on standards-based curriculum and instruction, that achievement tests today are requiring students to know, use, and apply information in more complex ways than were required some 20 or 30 years ago. If this is the case, then it seems that students would benefit from practice with this kind of thinking. To help students perform better on today's high-stakes tests, teachers should give students a range of opportunities to think—including knowledge questions as well as higher-order questions.

Implication: Teachers should purposefully plan and ask questions that require students to engage in higher-level thinking. Teachers should also help students become familiar with the different levels of thinking and help them be aware of the kind of thinking required by the question. Make visible

Research Finding #3: Not all students are accountable to respond to all questions. Teachers frequently call on volunteers, and these volunteers constitute a select group of students.

A. Well-Meaning Teacher calls on volunteers to answer questions—a time-honored approach in many classrooms. Researchers have used the term target students to identify those who dominate classroom discussion and recitations. In one study of fourth through eighth graders, target students talked more than three times as often as their classmates; 25 percent of the students never participated at all (Sadker & Sadker, 1985).

The presence of target students in most classrooms is particularly troubling in light of another research finding, that "students who regularly asked and answered questions did better on subsequent achievement tests than students who did not" (Strother, 1989). In this disparity between current practice and best practice, teachers are compelled to ask: How can we give all our students the opportunity to ask and answer questions, to participate in discussions and recitations, and to think out loud?

Implication: Teachers, not students, should usually decide who will answer questions. Teachers should use strategies that give every student an opportunity to respond. *They should also establish classroom norms indicating that every student deserves an opportunity to answer questions and that all students' answers are important. This will help the most verbal students monitor their own talking and allow other students an opportunity to respond to teacher questions.*

Research Finding #4: Teachers typically wait less than one second after asking a question before calling on a student to answer (Wait Time 1). They wait even less time (usually 0 seconds) before speaking after a student has answered (Wait Time 2).

Well-Meaning, like most of us, has established a fast-paced pattern for classroom questioning. Her intention is to keep students engaged by having little "down time" in a questioning episode. Unfortunately, her rapid-fire pace results in just the opposite—students who are not engaged and not thinking deeply about the content.

Research findings on the effects of Wait Time 1 and Wait Time 2 are consistently positive. When teachers pause for three to five seconds—both after asking a question and after hearing an answer—more students participate in class discussion, their answers are longer and of higher quality, and achievement improves on cognitively complex measures. Researchers have identified other benefits as well (see Chapter 4 for a more in-depth discussion of wait time and its effects).

Several studies indicate, however, that teachers rarely pause after asking questions or getting responses. In our own study, for example (Appalachia Educational Laboratory, 1994), we found that after teachers posed questions, they waited more than three seconds for a response less than 12 percent of the time. After students answered, teachers waited three seconds or more less than one percent of the time. And after more than 90 percent of student answers, teachers waited no time at all, frequently interrupting the student's answer.

Implication: Silence can be golden! Both Wait Times 1 and 2 promote student thinking and foster more students' formulating answers to more questions.

Research Finding #5: Teachers often accept incorrect answers without probing; they frequently answer their own questions.

Look again at how Well-Meaning responds to students whose answers are incomplete or incorrect. She might say "OK" and redirect the answer to another student. Many of us are reluctant to provide feedback to students who give less than correct answers; even fewer of us are willing to stick with that student—and provide prompts—to help the student complete a response to a question we've asked. It is rare to find a teacher who asks a student to explain his or her answer, give an example, or provide a rationale.

Several studies have confirmed that nearly half of student answers are at a different cognitive level than the teacher question, yet teachers generally accept these answers as sufficient without probing or prompting correct responses. Probing, however, is positively correlated with increased student achievement, as reported by Ornstein (1988) in a review of research about effective questioning practice.

Implication: In classrooms where the norm is that every student is capable of giving complete and correct answers, teachers provide prompts, when necessary, to help students give correct answers. When students give either incomplete or incorrect responses, teachers should seek to understand those answers more completely by gently guiding student thinking with appropriate probes.

Research Finding #6: Students ask very few content-related questions.

Well-Meaning's behavior mirrors that of most classroom teachers. The need to "cover the material" means that we cannot take the time for student questions. They might get us "off track." Indeed, in classrooms where teachers are posing two to three questions per minute, there's hardly a place for student questions anyway.

Many authors have written persuasively about how questions are essential to learning. For example, Neil Postman (1979) writes, "All our knowledge results from questions, which is another way of saying that question-asking is our most important intellectual tool" (p. 140). In a similar vein, Morgan and Saxton (1991) write, "Learning springs from curiosity—the need to know" (p. 18). They have proposed a taxonomy of student engagement, in which the asking of a question about the content demonstrates a higher level of engagement. In their framework, when students are extremely interested and engaged with a topic, they need to think about it, challenge the teacher, challenge their own ideas, and consider different points of view. Only at these higher levels of engagement, they contend, do students ask questions about the content.

Implication: If we teachers believe that student questions are essential to their deep engagement with, and learning of, a particular content, teachers will value student questions, help students learn to formulate good questions, and make time for student questions.

Commitment to Quality Questioning Is a Journey

Most teachers with whom we've worked over the years agree that we know much more about quality questions and questioning than we put into practice. In fact, at the beginning of our sessions on effective questioning, we ask participants to reflect on gaps between research and practice in five key areas and to identify reasons why we don't always follow best practice. (For a summary of responses from one of our trainings, see pp. 17-18.) Without fail, the following issues emerge as barriers to best practices.

- Content coverage
- Time constraints
- Habit or tradition
- A felt need to maintain "control" of class
- Ease for teacher
- Not wanting to embarrass students

Follow-up discussion about responses to the questions usually leads into a consideration of the culture of contemporary schools. Participants almost always agree that much of what drives individuals in schools today is a felt need to "get through" the overwhelming expectations that others set for them. For teachers, it's the pressure to cover the curriculum, to place checkmarks beside state or district standards or objectives, to prepare students for high-stakes tests. For students, it's pressure to get through the school year, to graduate, to meet parental expectations regarding postsecondary plans. So much gets lost in this press to meet other folks' expectations: the passion for teaching and learning, the excitement and energy needed to move from the routine and mundane to the relevant and important.

How can we move beyond these feelings of bewilderment, helplessness, and stress? By reclaiming our professional right and responsibility to teach all of our students what they need to know—and to teach in a manner that optimizes student engagement and personal responsibility for learning. We believe that a renewed commitment to quality questions and questioning has high potential for enabling and supporting us in this journey. And changing our questioning behaviors *is* a journey, a process that can occur over time when individuals develop the will and the skill—and when they have an appropriate framework and support. The remaining chapters in this book provide a roadmap for individuals and groups who are ready to embark on this exciting journey.

Why Does a Gap Exist Between Research and Practice?
Interview Design Questions and Reponses from Practitioners

When we conduct workshops on effective questioning, we often pose five questions that overview the major content of the workshop. We use Interview Design (a technique described in Chapter 3) as a way of actively engaging all workshop participants in answering all questions. The following is a summary of responses from teachers and administrators attending a workshop in Greensburg, Pennsylvania. The responses are typical of those we encounter in workshops throughout the United States. As you read the questions and responses, what common themes emerge? Do you understand better why our classroom practice doesn't always match exemplary research-based practice?

Question 1: Research reports that 75 to 80 percent of the questions posed in both elementary and secondary classrooms are at the *recall* or *memory* level. In your opinion, what are the three or four most important factors contributing to this situation?

- Coverage of content and textbook (time and planning)
- Recall questions are easier to ask (provides more teacher control)
- Schools are driven by curriculum, state standards, and state tests
- Society sees learning as knowing facts
- Tradition. This is the way teachers have been trained; it's "what we know"
- Lack of teacher knowledge and skills
- Easier to assess

Question 2: Research reports that most teachers call on students perceived as high achievers more frequently than they call on low achievers. What do you believe to be the two or three overriding reasons for this teacher behavior?

- Time constraints
- It's easier on the teacher
- Provides reinforcement of what's been taught
- Helps teachers feel successful
- More likely to get a serious (not silly) response
- Don't want to embarrass students who don't know the answers
- Lack of patience

Question 3: Research reports that when teachers ask questions of students, they typically wait one second or less for students to begin their responses. Why do you think teachers allow students so little time to begin their responses? Suggest two or three possible explanations.

- Silence (waiting) is uncomfortable
- Lack of time—there's so much you want to accomplish in a period
- Classroom management; can't allow much "down time"
- Need to keep things moving
- Get caught up in the excitement of the lesson
- Impatient teachers
- May not realize you're not giving wait time
- Need to keep students active and engaged

Question 4: Research reports that teachers frequently give a student the answer to a question that the student does not answer correctly or immediately. Can you suggest two or three reasons why many teachers provide the answer rather than attempt to elicit a correct response from the student?

- Time management—the curriculum is "full;" the lesson is packed
- Administrators expect to hear the answer given immediately after the question
- We're uncomfortable with wait time and silence
- Don't want to embarrass students
- Teachers have an expectation that the correct answer needs to be heard
- Lack of teacher ability to probe
- Depends on student ability level
- Students value teachers' answers more than student answers

Question 5: Research reports that students ask less than five percent of the questions in both elementary and secondary classrooms. Why do students initiate so few questions? Offer three or four hypotheses.

- Time is limited
- Afraid of embarrassment
- Students don't know how or don't feel comfortable asking
- Classrooms are teacher-driven versus student-centered
- Teacher is the authority; their role is to question

Questions for Reflection

Thinking, Learning, and Achievement:
How Can Quality Questioning Transform Classrooms?

This tool for self-reflection includes reminders of classroom practices that support effective questioning.

Classroom Design	Questions for Reflection
Use classroom norms to help students understand the role of questions and questioning in their learning.	Does the culture of my classroom support quality questioning? • Have I formulated a set of norms that will support a culture of inquiry and thoughtful dialogue? • Have I presented these norms to my students and provided them opportunities to think about how these norms can support their learning?
Use structures to scaffold new student behaviors.	Are there structures in place to support students as they learn to be more fully engaged in classroom discourse? • Do I use a variety of formats to engage students in the answering of questions? • Have students learned the rules and procedures that accompany these formats? • Do I use visual and auditory signals to facilitate smooth transitions from one format to another?
Align teacher and student roles and responsibilities with new vision for teaching and learning.	Is my classroom student-centered; that is, do I maintain a focus on students, as opposed to content *per se*? • Do I see myself as a facilitator of student learning, rather than a content expert to whom students turn for all knowledge? • Are students responsible for their learning and accountable for constructing their own answers to all questions and for making personal meaning from content? • Do students approach learning as a collaborative endeavor, in which they work together and with the teacher to achieve learning goals?
Students (and teacher) value quality questions and questioning and are aware of "good practice."	To what extent do you and your students possess a shared understanding of what good questions and questioning processes look and sound like? • Do you understand the implications of research on questioning for your classroom? • Have you talked with your students about the value of questions and questioning in their learning—and provided a forum for them to think and talk about this topic? • Have you taught your students rules and procedures associated with quality questioning?

References

Appalachia Educational Laboratory. (1994). *Questioning and Understanding to Improve Learning and Thinking (QUILT): The evaluation results. A proposal to the National Diffusion Network (NDN) documenting the effectiveness of the QUILT professional development program.* (ERIC Document Reproduction Service No. ED403230)

Covey, S. R. (1990). *The seven habits of highly effective people.* New York: Simon & Schuster.

Deal, T., & Peterson, K. (1998). *Shaping school culture.* San Francisco: Jossey-Bass.

Gall, M. (1971). The use of questions in teaching. *Review of Educational Research, 40,* 707-721.

Gall, M. D., Ward, B. A., Berliner, D. C., Cahen, L. S., Winne, P. H., Elashoff, J. D., & Stanton, G. C. (1978). Effects of questioning techniques and recitation on student learning. *American Educational Research Journal, 15,* 175-199.

Gall, M. (1984). Synthesis of research on teachers' questioning. *Educational Leadership, 42*(3), 40-47.

Harmin, M. (1994). *Inspiring active learning: A handbook for teachers.* Alexandria, VA: Association for Supervision and Curriculum Development.

Hunkins, F. P. (1995). *Teaching thinking through effective questioning* (2nd ed.). Boston: Christopher-Gordon Publishers.

Marzano, R. J., Pickering , D. J., & Pollock, J. E. (2001). *Classroom instruction that works: Research-based strategies for increasing student achievement.* Alexandria, VA: Association for Supervision and Curriculum Development.

Morgan, N., & Saxton, J. (1991). *Teaching, questioning, and learning.* London: Routledge.

Ornstein, A. C. (1988, February). Questioning: The essence of good teaching—part II. *NASSP Bulletin.*

Perkins, D. (1992). *Smart schools: From training memories to educating minds.* New York: Free Press.

Postman, N. (1979). *Teaching as a conserving activity.* New York: Dell, Laurel Press.

Redfield, D. L., & Rousseau, E. W. (1981). A meta-analysis of experimental research on teacher questioning behavior. *Review of Educational Research, 51,* 237-245.

Rowe, M. B. (1972, April). *Wait time and rewards as instructional variables: Their influence in language, logic, and fate control.* Paper presented at the National Association for Research in Science Teaching, Chicago, IL. (ERIC Document Reproduction Service No. ED061103)

Rowe, M. B. (1986, January-February). Wait time: Slowing down may be a way of speeding up! *Journal of Teacher Education, 37*(1), 43-50.

Sadker, D., & Sadker, M. (1985). Is the OK classroom OK? *Phi Delta Kappan, 66*(5), 358-361.

Strother, D. B. (1989). Developing thinking skills through questioning. *Phi Delta Kappan, 71*(4), 324-327.

Susskind, E. (1979, Summer). Encouraging teachers to encourage children's curiosity: A pivotal competence. *Journal of Clinical Child Psychology, 8,* 101-106.

Thompson, C. L., & Zeuli, J. S. (1999). The frame and the tapestry: Standards-based reform and professional development. In L. Darling-Hammond & G. Sykes (Eds.), *Teaching as the learning profession: Handbook of policy and practice* (pp. 341-375). New York: Teachers College Press.

Walsh, J. A., & Sattes, B. D. (2003). *Questioning and Understanding to Improve Learning and Thinking: Teacher Manual* (2nd ed.). Charleston, WV: AEL.

Wells, G. (2001). The case for dialogic inquiry. In G. Wells (Ed.), *Action, talk, and text: Learning and teaching through inquiry* (pp. 171-194). New York: Teachers College Press.

Wiggins, G., & McTighe, J. (2000). *Understanding by design.* Alexandria, VA: Association for Supervision and Curriculum Development.

Wilen, W. A., & Clegg, A. A., Jr. (1986, Spring). Effective questions and questioning: A research review. *Theory and Research in Social Education, 14*(2), 153-61.

Chapter 2:
What Are the Characteristics of Quality Questions? Formulating Questions That Trigger Thinking

Focus Questions

What are the characteristics of a quality question—one that focuses attention, stimulates thinking, and results in real learning?

What kinds of questions hold the greatest potential for scaffolding student thinking to higher cognitive levels?

How can we help our students understand the relationship between quality questions and learning?

Teachers who believe questions are tools for actively engaging students in learning dedicate time and effort to preparing questions. They pose purposeful questions that help students make meaning of new concepts and ideas, thus demonstrating the relationship between quality questions and thinking and learning.

Margaret Allen, director of professional development in Montgomery County Public Schools in Alabama, has "come to believe that good questions can be the fuel for the learning process." She views question formulation as a powerful cognitive process:

> To form a good question takes work; it takes thought, skill, and practice. Questions are opportunities to open up learning, to connect it to prior learning. Children have the capacity for this connection; you just have to find the right ways to help them do it.

"Effective questions help provide the scaffolding for student learning," observes one teacher. "But formulating these questions is hard work; it requires me to grapple with what's important about the content. I ask myself: What questions will 'hook' my students' interest and get them thinking about and learning the content and skills on which they'll be tested?" This experienced teacher considers both the curriculum and the students. This approach increases his professional learning about how to connect students with curriculum in pursuit of standards and goals.

Questions Can Scaffold Learning

Right now an important idea in reading is the concept of scaffolding. If there's one thing we know, questions help you scaffold. As I look at scaffolding, I think of house painters. They have to use a ladder or some kind of scaffolding, or they wouldn't be able to reach the high places, and their task would be half finished. Similarly, we as teachers can use questions as a kind of scaffolding to help students reach higher levels of thinking and learning.

We are able to understand where kids are . . . and provide them with the help and support that they need to become independent learners. We intervene when necessary and allow freedom when they are able to function without our assistance. By using scaffolding, we demonstrate that we are perceptive enough to know what to do to help our students become independent learners.

Robert Iuzzolino, Director of Curriculum Services, Westmoreland Intermediate Unit, Pennsylvania

Stuart Greenberg, deputy director for the Eastern Regional Reading First Technical Assistance Center, talks about the relationship between quality questions and the improvement of thinking and reading:

> As teachers ask good questions, they are modeling thinking for students. To ask good questions, teachers are required to have in-depth knowledge; additionally, they have to preview the text and then generate questions that will take students to more complex thinking. Graphic organizers, which are another way to promote thinking, are more of a passive way. In the asking of questions, teachers are thinking actively and helping students be active thinkers.

Greenberg believes that quality questions help students think about what they read—and do something with it.

J. T. Dillon (1983, 1988), a longtime student of effective questioning, uses the term *educative* to characterize questions that advance learning and thinking. In Dillon's view, these questions are purposeful, engaging, and consequential. They are aligned with learning goals, awaken student curiosity and class participation, and result in desired learning outcomes (Anderson & Krathwohl, 2001; Bloom, 1987). But what criteria can we use in formulating effective, productive, or **quality questions?** We identify four characteristics of quality questions. Such questions (1) promote one or more carefully defined instructional purposes, (2) focus on important content, (3) facilitate thinking at a stipulated cognitive level, and (4) communicate clearly what is being asked.

Criteria associated with all four dimensions of a quality question, and a scale for self-assessment of teacher questions, are presented in Figure 2.1, Rubric for Formulating and Assessing Quality Questions. We will refer to this rubric throughout the chapter and encourage you to use it as a tool in your own question formulation.

Figure 2.1

Rubric for Formulating and Assessing Quality Questions*

Score	Purpose	Content Focus	Cognitive Level	Wording and Syntax (Communication)
3	*Directly* relates to one or more learner objectives Challenges students to think about concepts and to formulate personal responses (gets students' attention and interest) Has a clear and important role and function in the lesson	Elicits knowledge related to the concepts being studied Elicits knowledge that *all* students have had the opportunity to learn Logically and directly builds upon previous questions and answers in the lesson or unit (i.e., is properly sequenced)	Engages student thinking at a cognitive level that is clearly specified and modeled by the teacher Includes words or phrases that cue students to respond at the intended cognitive level Asks students to process knowledge *at the highest level*, according to their readiness Prompts students to see relationships and patterns, demonstrate understandings, and make connections	Uses vocabulary that is appropriate to (a) the age and grade level of students and (b) the content or discipline being studied Uses words that are unambiguous and precise Structures, organizes, and sequences words and phrases to make the question clear and to help the student understand what is expected in a response Uses (a) the fewest possible number of words and (b) the simplest possible structure
2	*Somewhat* relates to one or more learner objectives *To some degree,* challenges students to think about concepts (gets students' attention) Has a role and function in the lesson	Elicits knowledge related to the concepts being studied, at least in part Elicits knowledge that *most* students have had the opportunity to learn Builds upon previous questions and answers	Engages student thinking Includes few words to cue students to respond at the intended cognitive level Asks students to process knowledge Prompts students to see connections	Uses vocabulary that is *mostly* appropriate to the students and the content Uses words that are fairly clear and precise Gives students a *general* idea of what is expected in a response Uses relatively few words and a fairly simple structure
1	It is not clearly connected to lesson purpose	Elicits knowledge covered in the text but not already learned by all students	Lacks clarity as to expected level of cognition to be exhibited in student answer	Uses vocabulary inappropriate to students and content; includes ambiguous words or awkward phrasing

* This scoring rubric has been designed for use by teachers seeking to improve the quality of the questions they pose in the classroom. As such, it is intended for self-assessment and improvement only. This rubric is generic and may be adapted by individual teachers to specific content areas and/or grade levels.

Quality Questions Are Purposeful

As the rubric indicates, the purpose of a question depends on the instructional objective. In thinking about purpose, it is most helpful to consider the context in which the question(s) will be posed. Two typical classroom contexts for questioning are recitation and discussion. The more familiar of the two, *recitation,* involves the teacher in every interchange. He or she poses a question and, after student response, confirms the rightness or wrongness of the answer. Recitations usually find the teacher speaking in questions; they may pose up to 50 questions during a one-hour class. In contrast, students speak in short, factual answers—and look to the teacher for an evaluation of their correctness. Questions posed in recitation are usually low-level questions, asking students to remember or recall facts, provide definitions, or demonstrate comprehension. Rarely do recitation questions engage students in thinking deeply about an issue.

Discussion, on the other hand, may be less familiar. Researchers have found true classroom discussions occur infrequently in elementary and secondary school classrooms—about four to eight percent of the time (Dillon, 1984). In a true discussion, a teacher might pose a single, provocative, open-ended question and ask other questions only for clarification. The teacher assures that all students have an opportunity to contribute, provide evidence for their statements, and stay on topic. Students don't wait for the teacher's permission to speak and they don't look to the teacher for assessment of responses; they engage in dialogue with one another, listen respectfully, and make their own evaluations.

As you might imagine, the purposes of questions in these two contexts are very different. *Recitation* questions might be posed for the following purposes:

- To review before a test
- To see if students have read and understood a passage
- To check on completion and/or comprehension of homework
- To assess what students know about a topic—either before, during, or after instruction
- To cue students on important content
- To get students to talk (especially in cooperative groups)
- To provide opportunities for drill and practice
- To model good questioning for students

Questions that promote discussion might be posed for the following purposes:

- To afford students practice in thinking out loud
- To encourage students to hear and respect diverse points of view
- To help students work out their own understanding of a topic
- To improve listening skills
- To provide an opportunity for students to speculate, formulate hypotheses, and offer evidence to support their ideas
- To allow students time and opportunity to reflect upon and verbalize their own beliefs on a topic
- To encourage students to make connections that will help them move information to long-term memory
- To create opportunities for students to transfer learning to different contexts or situations

When we say a quality question must be purposeful, then, we mean that the teacher will have formulated it after asking herself, "What, ultimately, is my purpose in asking a question at this time?"

Consider the questions posed by Jane Hashey of Vestal, New York, to her eighth-grade English class as they finished the third chapter of *The Outsiders*. A character in the novel has been killed in self-defense. Jane asked the standard questions ("What happened?" and "Why did he do that?" and so forth) to see if the students had read the passage and understood what they read. Then she "flipped the switch" and asked, "Well, is it ever okay to kill someone?" The energy level in the room visibly increased as Jane moved from the "boring," low-level questions to one that required her students to think—a question for which they couldn't look to the text for an answer; one for which there was no single right answer. Her question truly grabbed the attention of her students. It got them to think, talk, and listen.

In this example, the initial questions served an important purpose—they set the stage for the later question by making sure all the students understood the text, were clear about what happened in the story, and could "ease into" the discussion that followed. Jane's purpose in asking the final question was to give students an opportunity to think about a serious subject, consider what society's reaction to such an event should be, and listen to one another's points of view as they processed their own thoughts and beliefs. Her questions were purposeful—the first step toward quality.

When teachers are clear about the purposes of questions, they can better assess student responses. For example, if the designated purpose of a discussion is to use evidence in support of one's viewpoint, the teacher can hold students to this standard, rather than allowing undisciplined or unbridled talk. It is also critical that students know the purpose of a questioning episode so that they can monitor their own participation and performance.

Quality Questions Have a Clear Content Focus

Once teachers have specified the purpose(s) for their question, they must wrestle with the question "On what specific content do I want to pose a question to students?" This aspect is perhaps the most difficult of question design today. Not only do teachers confront an exponentially increasing knowledge base, but they must also prepare students for high-stakes tests mandated by state and federal policymakers. They need to consider the alignment of their content to these standards. So it is more important than ever that teachers have clear criteria in mind as they decide what is most critical for students to know, then formulate pivotal questions based on these decisions.

The choices for focus are limitless. In our workshops, we typically ask teachers to read a short passage from a children's novel, *Charlotte's Web.* Early in the novel, a young farm girl's father allows her to take the runt pig as a pet, saving the pig from a certain and premature death. We ask teachers to think about the passage, select the most important content focus around which to pose a question for discussion, and be ready to tell why that focus is important. The resultant topics are always diverse: the concept of responsibility; the life cycle of farm animals; the roles, responsibilities, and relationships of family members; innate behaviors vs. learned behaviors; the function of pets in our society; caring for others; and so forth.

Frameworks Can Help Prioritize Content

With so many choices, how can a teacher prioritize content to determine what is most important? In *Understanding by Design*, Grant Wiggins and Jay McTighe (1998) introduce a model for thinking about "what's worth teaching." They advocate what they call a *backward design process*, which consists of three stages: identify the desired result—what you want students to know, understand, and be able to do; determine what will constitute acceptable evidence of student learning; and plan learning experiences and instruction accordingly.

We focus here on only the first stage—identifying the desired result. Wiggins and McTighe present a helpful framework for keeping the end result in mind while establishing curricular priorities, "given that there typically is more content than can reasonably be addressed" (p. 9). Their framework can be visualized as three nested spheres, each representing a different kind of knowledge. The outermost tier encompasses *knowledge with which it is worth being familiar*—information that teachers present because it is part of a shared cultural context. E. D. Hirsh's *Cultural Literacy* provides examples of this category of information.

The second layer of knowledge, nested within the first, represents content— *what is important to know and be able to do.* This includes the "prerequisite knowledge [facts, concepts, principles] and skills [concepts, principles, processes]

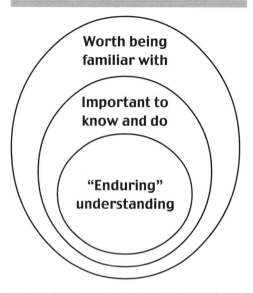

Worth being
familiar with

Important to
know and do

"Enduring"
understanding

Reprinted, with permission, from Grant Wiggins and Jay McTighe, *Understanding by Design* (Alexandria, VA: Association for Supervision and Curriculum Development, 1998), p. 10.

needed by students for them to successfully accomplish key performances" (Wiggins & McTighe, 1998, p. 10). Students need to master this content in order to meet standards, perform at an established level of proficiency on a standardized test or assessment, or, more important, function successfully in society.

The innermost tier, nested in the heart of the framework, represents *enduring understandings* that anchor the course or a unit within a course. These are the big ideas and important understandings that we want students to retain long after they have forgotten many of the details. This kind of knowledge endures when students connect personal experiences and interests to context and content knowledge. Using the schema offered by Wiggins and McTighe, teachers can formulate questions that are intentionally aligned with content objectives *and* designed to help students make significant connections in a given area of study. In other words, three considerations should go into thinking about content focus: (1) selecting a "big idea" worthy of discussion, (2) making sure it connects to the standards required and measured by the state in which students are tested, and (3) tying it to the needs and interests of your own group of students.

The
Subject

Personal
Knowledge

Other
Subjects

Adapted from the work of Leila Christenbury and Patricia P. Kelly, *Questioning: A Path to Critical Thinking* (1983).

Another framework that is helpful in selecting content focus for questions comes from the work of Christenbury and Kelly (1983). Their *questioning circle* calls attention to the relationship between what they term *matter* (the subject matter), *personal reality* (student knowledge derived from experience), and *external reality* (knowledge from other content areas and the outside world). We call these domains *the subject, personal knowledge,* and *other subjects.*

As the Venn diagram illustrates, teacher questions can fall into (1) a single domain such as personal knowledge, (2) two overlapping domains, such as personal knowledge and the subject, or (3) all three domains. Christenbury and Kelly believe teachers should use all three types of questions. But they suggest that the most powerful or "dense" questions are found in the intersection of the three areas of the Venn diagram: the subject under study, the individual's life outside of school, and other subject areas as well as the real world. For examples of all three types of questions (single-domain, overlap, and dense), see Figure 2.2, Questioning Circle: Sample Questions.

Figure 2.2

Questioning Circle
(Sample Questions)

Example 1. AEL science specialist Anita Deck offers the following questions for use in a middle school science classroom. The lesson purpose is to introduce an environmental science unit. The initial assignment was to read *The Lorax* by Dr. Seuss.

Single-Domain Questions *(white area of Venn diagram)*
The Subject: What problems occurred in the Lorax's world after the Once-ler arrived?
Personal Knowledge: Under what circumstances would you support legislation to preserve and protect the environment at the expense of human needs?
Other Subjects: How does the loss of trees affect the environment, particularly the animals and birds?

Overlap Questions *(gray area of Venn diagram)*
The Subject/Personal Knowledge: If you had the only Truffula seed given to you, what would you do?
Personal Knowledge/Other Subjects: How do you balance your need for the many things made from wood and the need to maintain forests?
The Subject/Other Subjects: How does the fate of the Truffula Village relate to current predictions about Earth's environment?

Dense Questions *(black area of Venn diagram)*
The Subject/Personal Knowledge/Other Subjects: "Sustainable development" is defined as meeting the needs of the present without reducing the ability of people to meet their needs in the future. Many human activities, like the Once-ler's business, are planned for the short term (perhaps a few years). Why is the practice of sustainable development desirable?

Example 2. Nancy Abramovic, a third-grade language arts teacher in Pennsylvania, read aloud to her class from *The Orphan Train Quartet: A Family Apart* by Joan Lowery Nixon. In the story, six siblings live with their widowed mother in the slums of New York City in 1856. The mother makes the ultimate sacrifice of love and sends them west on the orphan train for a better life. Nancy posed the following questions for discussion after reading the first seven chapters, stopping just before the children reach their destination of St. Joseph, Missouri.

Single-Domain Questions *(white area of Venn diagram)*
The Subject: What is the problem the characters are trying to solve?
Personal Knowledge: Have you ever wanted something that didn't belong to you?
Other Subjects: What is a slum?

Overlap Questions *(gray area of Venn diagram)*
The Subject/Personal Knowledge: Use a Venn diagram to compare and contrast your life with the Kelly children's lives. Write at least three ways your lives are alike and three ways they are different.
Personal Knowledge/Other Subjects: Have you ever taken something that didn't belong to you? If so, what was the consequence?
The Subject/Other Subjects: In the mid to late1800s, what happened to children who were "copper stealers?"

Dense Questions *(black area of Venn diagram)*
The Subject/Personal Knowledge/Other Subjects: Would it ever be right to take something that is not yours, as Mike did when he took the money that had been stolen from the train passengers? If so, when? If not, why not?

Example 3. The following questions are related to the novel *My Brother Sam Is Dead* by James Lincoln Collier and Christopher Collier. They were suggested by Carla Breeding, a Kentucky seventh-grade teacher featured on the Video Journal of Education series in *Questioning to Stimulate Learning and Thinking: Secondary Level.*

Single-Domain Questions *(white area of Venn diagram)*
The Subject: Why does Sam come home?
Personal Knowledge: Can you think of any situation that would cause you to want to fight for what's right?
Other Subjects: Why were the people who lived in the American colonies fighting the British?

Overlap Questions *(gray area of Venn diagram)*
The Subject/Personal Knowledge: Do Sam's reasons for wanting to go to war seem convincing to you?
Personal Knowledge/Other Subjects: Given the situation at the time, would you have decided to go to war?
The Subject/Other Subjects: What choices did a boy Sam's age have at that time? What were the factors that needed to be weighed before making such a decision?

Dense Questions *(black area of Venn diagram)*
The Subject/Personal Knowledge/Other Subjects: When, do you think you should fight for what you think is right, even if your family does not believe that you should?

Quality Questions Engage Students at Varied and Appropriate Cognitive Levels

Questions are tools for both information seeking and information processing (Hunkins, 1995). Hence, as we formulate our questions, we need to be clear not only about the content we expect in student answers, but also about the kind of thinking or processing for which we'll hold students accountable. A variety of tools exist for helping identify and distinguish different kinds of thinking or cognition. The most widely known is Bloom's Taxonomy, which was revised in 2001. Because the original version is already familiar to teachers, and because it is such a powerful tool for formulating quality questions, this chapter discusses the recently revised version of Bloom's Taxonomy in some detail. Other, simplified classification systems are also discussed (Marzano's, Gallagher & Aschner's, one commonly used by reading teachers, and a three-level system we devised ourselves).

Bloom's Taxonomy (Revised)

The original Bloom's Cognitive Taxonomy was the product of a long-term endeavor by college and university examiners to create a schema for classifying intended student learning outcomes so that examiners at different institutions could exchange test items, testing procedures, and ideas about testing (Anderson & Krathwohl, 2001). The 1956 publication of the *Taxonomy of Educational Objectives: Handbook I: Cognitive Domain* introduced this framework to a wider audience, including K-12 educators (Bloom, 1987).

Most teachers can name the six levels of the original Bloom Taxonomy: *knowledge, comprehension, application, analysis, synthesis,* and *evaluation.* Many schools and districts require teachers to use the Bloom Taxonomy in formulating objectives and planning lessons. In response to increased pressure to help students think at higher levels, many textbook publishers use it to classify questions appearing in teachers' editions.

For many years, we presented the Bloom Taxonomy in our workshops on effective questioning, and participating teachers valued the opportunity to renew their understanding of it. Many, at our suggestion, taught it to their students. They reported this to be a powerful tool for helping students understand what teacher questions and standardized test questions were asking of them, and how to formulate their own questions. Our experience confirms Francis Hunkins' contention that "as we involve students with question types, we focus on educating students' minds rather than their memories" (1995, p. 66).

In 2001, *A Taxonomy for Learning, Teaching, and Assessing: A Revision of Bloom's Taxonomy of Educational Objectives* was published. Like the original *Handbook,* this volume was the culmination of a multiyear collaboration among scholars—cognitive psychologists, curriculum theorists, instructional researchers, and testing and assessment specialists. Their avowed purpose was to (1) "refocus educators' attention on the value of the original *Handbook*" and (2) "incorporate new knowledge and thought into the framework" (Anderson & Krathwohl, pp. xxi-xxii).

The most significant change to Bloom's original taxonomy is the move from a one-dimensional to a two-dimensional scheme for classification. Whereas Bloom focused on the cognitive dimension, the revised taxonomy incorporates both a *cognitive process dimension* and a *knowledge dimension*. (The Taxonomy Table, Figure 2.3, illustrates how these two dimensions intersect.) The revision also incorporates current research and understandings of cognitive and classroom processes. It is beyond the scope of this book to provide a detailed comparison of the original and revised taxonomies; however, we will highlight major changes for the benefit of readers who are schooled in the original.

Figure 2.3

The Taxonomy Table

The Knowledge Dimension	The Cognitive Process Dimension					
	1 Remember	2 Understand	3 Apply	4 Analyze	5 Evaluate	6 Create
A. Factual Knowledge						
B. Conceptual Knowledge						
C. Procedural Knowledge						
D. Metacognitive Knowledge						

Reproduced, with permission, from Lorin W. Anderson and David R. Krathwohl, *A Taxonomy for Learning, Teaching, and Assessing: A Revision of Bloom's Taxonomy of Educational Objectives.* (Boston: Allyn and Bacon, 2001), p. 28.

The Cognitive Process Dimension

The six categories comprising the cognitive process dimension are comparable to the original six cognitive levels. These updated categories, in order of increasing complexity, are *remember* (knowledge), *understand* (comprehension), *apply* (application), *analyze* (analysis), *evaluate* (evaluation), and *create* (synthesis).

Readers familiar with the original Bloom Taxonomy will immediately note three differences. First, the new levels are expressed as verbs instead of nouns (for example, *apply* in lieu of *application*). This change is consistent with the view that thinking is an action verb. Second, a number of the roots are changed. For example, *remember* is distinguishable from *knowledge*, the title of the newly created second dimension of the revised taxonomy. Third, the order of the last two levels has been reversed; that is, *evaluate* precedes *create*.

The authors of the revised Bloom Taxonomy also added a new feature: for each of the six cognitive dimensions, they provide two or more specific cognitive processes (e.g., recalling, classifying, critiquing), each expressed as a verb. The addition of these 19 clearly defined cognitive processes makes the revised taxonomy more definitive and robust. It also makes the taxonomy even more useful to teachers as they formulate questions that engage student thinking at all levels. (See Figure 2.4 for a detailed look at the cognitive process dimension.)

Note that only one of the revised taxonomy's six categories *(remember)* is devoted to retention of knowledge. The other five *(understand, apply, analyze, evaluate,* and *create)* relate to an individual's ability to transfer knowledge—to make sense of and be able to use what they learn. Instruction and assessment in K-12 schools usually emphasize *retention* rather than *transfer*. Most educators give lip service to the need to move students beyond such rote learning, but few actually provide students with opportunities to make personal meaning out of information. Instructional theorists who advocate constructivist learning emphasize the importance of student engagement in active cognitive processing.

Mayer (1999) writes that when students actively process incoming information, they organize it so that it makes sense and they integrate it with existing knowledge. He contrasts this with rote learning, in which students are exhorted to add new information to their memories, layer upon layer. We must move students beyond the *remember* level of cognition if we are to help them make sense of incoming information.

The authors of the revised Bloom Taxonomy subscribe to a constructivist approach and argue that the cognitive process dimension can assist teachers in planning objectives, activities, and assessments that promote meaningful learning. It can also help in formulating questions that promote such learning. Let's take a closer look at the six components of this dimension, along with sample questions illustrating each.

Figure 2.4

The Cognitive Process Dimension

Categories & Cognitive Processes	Alternative Names	Definitions and Examples
1. Remember—Retrieve relevant knowledge from long-term memory		
1.1 Recognizing	Identifying	Locating knowledge in long-term memory that is consistent with presented material (e.g., Recognize the dates of important events in U.S. history)
1.2 Recalling	Retrieving	Retrieving relevant knowledge from long-term memory (e.g., Recall the dates of important events in U.S. history)
2. Understand—Construct meaning from instructional messages, including oral, written, and graphic communication		
2.1 Interpreting	Clarifying Paraphrasing Representing Translating	Changing from one form of representation (e.g., numerical) to another (e.g., verbal) (e.g., Paraphrase important speeches and documents)
2.2 Exemplifying	Illustrating Instantiating	Finding a specific example or illustration of a concept or principle (e.g., Give examples of various artistic painting styles)
2.3 Classifying	Categorizing Subsuming	Determining that something belongs to a catagory (e.g., Classify observed or described cases of mental disorders)
2.4 Summarizing	Abstracting Generalizing	Abstracting a general theme or major point(s) (e.g., Write a short summary of events portrayed on a videotape)
2.5 Inferring	Concluding Extrapolating Interpolating Predicting	Drawing a logical conclusion from presented information (e.g., In learning a foreign language, infer grammatical principles from examples)
2.6 Comparing	Contrasting Mapping Matching	Detecting correspondences between two ideas, objects, and the like (e.g., Compare historical events to contemporary situations)
2.7 Explaining	Constructing	Constructing a cause-and-effect model of a system (e.g., Explain the causes of important 18th-century events in France)
3. Apply—Carry out or use a procedure in a given situation		
3.1 Executing	Carrying out	Applying a procedure to a familiar task (e.g., Divide one whole number by another whole number, both with multiple digits)

3.2 Implementing	Using	Applying a procedure to an unfamiliar task (e.g., Use Newton's Second Law in situations in which it is appropriate)
4. Analyze—Break material into its constituent parts and determine how the parts relate to one another and to an overall structure or purpose		
4.1 Differentiating	Discriminating Distinguishing Focusing Selecting	Distinguishing relevant from irrelevant parts or important from unimportant parts of presented material (e.g., Distinguish between relevant and irrelevant numbers in a mathematical word problem)
4.2 Organizing	Finding coherence Integrating Outlining Parsing Structuring	Determine how elements fit or function within a structure (e.g., Structure evidence in a historical description into evidence for and against a particular historical explanation)
4.3 Attributing	Deconstructing	Determine a point of view, a bias, values, or intent underlying presented material (e.g., Determine the point of view of the author of an essay in terms of his or her political perspective)
5. Evaluate—Make judgments based on criteria and standards		
5.1 Checking	Coordinating Detecting Monitoring Testing	Detecting inconsistencies or fallacies within a process or product; determining whether a process or product has external consistency; determining the effectiveness of a procedure as it is being implemented (e.g., Determine if a scientist's conclusions follow from the raw data)
5.2 Critiquing	Judging	Determining inconsistencies between a product and external criteria; determining whether a product has external consistency; determining the appropriateness of a procedure for a given problem (e.g., Judge which of two methods is the best way to solve a given problem)
6. Create—Put elements together to form a coherent or functional whole; reorganize elements into a new pattern or structure		
6.1 Generating	Hypothesizing	Coming up with alternative hypotheses based on criteria (e.g., Generate hypotheses to account for an observed phenomenon)
6.2. Planning	Designing	Devising a procedure for accomplishing some task (e.g., Plan a research paper on a given historical topic)
6.3. Producing	Constructing	Inventing a product (e.g., Build habitats for a specific purpose)

Reproduced, with permission, from Lorin W. Anderson and David R. Krathwohl, *A Taxonomy for Learning, Teaching, and Assessing: A Revision of Bloom's Taxonomy of Educational Objectives* (Boston: Allyn and Bacon, 2001), p. 31.

1. Remember. Questions that ask students to recognize or recall information evoke the lowest level of cognitive processing, yet remembering is critical for meaningful learning and problem solving. Students must be able to retrieve information if they are to use it in more cognitively complex operations. The key is for teachers to embed such questions within the "larger task of constructing new knowledge or solving new problems" (Anderson & Krathwohl, 2001, pp. 68-69). The following questions exemplify remembering:

- What is the chemical expression or formula for *water?*

- Who was president of the United States at the time of the Louisiana Purchase?

2. Understand. A first step in helping students transfer memorized information to new situations is to facilitate connections between new knowledge and prior knowledge and experiences—or, as the authors of the revised taxonomy put it, "incoming knowledge is integrated with existing schemas and cognitive frameworks" (p. 70). Notice the cognitive processes associated with understanding: interpreting, exemplifying, classifying, summarizing, inferring, comparing, and explaining.

If a question is to move students beyond the first level of the cognitive process dimension (*remember*), it must include information that students did not encounter during initial instruction. It must require students to reach beyond memory alone to answer. Consider how these questions push students beyond the *remember* level.

- In what ways is water associated with satisfying the physical, emotional, and spiritual needs of human beings?

- Compare the circumstances surrounding the United States' acquisition of the Louisiana Purchase to those surrounding its purchase of Alaska.

3. Apply. The taxonomy distinguishes between two types of application: execution and implementation. Execution involves applying a procedure to a familiar task:

- Using the information provided on a U.S. map, estimate the length in miles of the Mississippi River.

- Find the northernmost point in the Louisiana Territory on the map, and tell me its longitude and latitude.

Implementation is more complex because it involves applying a procedure to an unfamiliar task and "requires some degree of understanding of the problem as well as of the solution procedure" (Anderson & Krathwohl, p. 77).

- Identify the U.S. cities you believe developed after the advent of rail travel.

- Assume that you lived in Washington, DC, in 1800 and planned to travel overland to New Orleans. What route and modes of transportation would you have employed to reach your destination in the shortest amount of time?

4. Analyze. Analysis involves breaking down a whole (idea or problem) into its component parts and determining how the parts are related one to another. Analysis is an important cognitive process for all disciplines. The following abilities are associated with analysis:

- Distinguishing fact from opinion, reality from fantasy
- Connecting conclusions with supportive statements
- Distinguishing relevant from extraneous information
- Determining the relationship between and among ideas
- Identifying unstated assumptions in a written or oral statement
- Finding evidence to support an author's purpose
- Distinguishing dominant from subordinate themes or ideas in literature, music, and other fields (Anderson & Krathwohl, 2001, pp. 79-80)

These are examples of analysis questions:

- What impact did the building of dams to generate hydroelectric power have upon the development of our nation?
- What evidence can you offer to support the contention that Thomas Jefferson was a risk taker?
- What are some of the primary themes in Lewis and Clark's journals?

5. Evaluate. Evaluation involves making a judgment based upon the application of a set of standards or criteria. The key to evaluation is the identification and use of standards or criteria. Some frequently used criteria are quality, effectiveness, efficiency, and consistency (Anderson & Krathwohl, 2001). These criteria may be either quantitative or qualitative.

The two cognitive processes associated with *evaluate* are checking (which involves making judgments about internal consistency), and critiquing (for which judgments are made based upon external criteria). The following questions would engage students in checking:

- Were the social policies of President Johnson's administration consistent with his voting record as a U.S. senator?
- Do the survey data we collected from parents in this school confirm our hypothesis about parental monitoring of their children's television viewing?

Questions that involve students in critiquing invite them to identify positive and negative aspects of a particular product or issue, or to look at the pro's and the con's. This cognitive process, which is closely associated with critical thinking, is embodied in the following questions:

- Which of these two paintings best represent impressionist art?

- Is NASA justified in abandoning the Hubble telescope?

The cognitive processes of *understand, analyze,* and *evaluate* are connected and are often used together, but the authors of the revised taxonomy suggest maintaining them as separate process categories. This allows teachers to differentiate a student's ability to evaluate from the student's ability to analyze or simply understand a given problem or issue (Anderson & Krathwohl, 2001, p. 80). *Evaluate,* like the four lower levels of cognitive processing *(remember, understand, apply,* and *analyze),* asks students to work with a set of elements that are a part of a given whole.

6. Create. The final cognitive process in the revised taxonomy engages students in putting together disparate parts to form a new whole. *Create* corresponds to "synthesis" in the original Bloom Taxonomy. The authors of the revised taxonomy place *create* at a higher level than *evaluate* because *create* is a cognitive process for which "the student must draw upon elements from many sources and put them together in a novel structure or pattern relative to his or her own prior knowledge. *Create* results in a new product that is something that can be observed and that is more than the students' beginning materials" (Anderson & Krathwohl, 2001, p. 65). For example:

- Design a security system that would protect the safety of all students in our school with minimal infringement on individual rights.

- Create a plan for water conservation that you believe you can "sell" to your peers.

While planning lessons, it is often appropriate to formulate questions at all six cognitive levels, relating the questions to both the essential question of a given unit and to lesson objectives. (See Figure 2.5 for examples of teacher-developed questions.)

A tool we find useful in question planning and formulation is the "Q-Card" on page 40. For each cognitive level, the Q-Card provides stems for questions (or teacher prompts), expected student performances, and suggested probes a teacher might use when student responses are incomplete or incorrect. The Q-Card is also helpful in processing student answers during the flow of a class. We encourage you to use this tool as you seek to become more intentional in formulating and assessing questions at all levels of cognition.

Figure 2.5

Lesson Planning
Sample Questions for All Six Cognitive Levels

Class: Mathematics, Grade 3

Objectives: (1) Students will be able to describe how addition and multiplication are similar. (2) Students will know the appropriate use of addition and multiplication.

Essential Question: Which is a better way of solving problems—addition or multiplication?

Focusing Question: How do you determine when to add and when to multiply?

Remember

1. How many 3's are you adding in 3 + 3 + 3 + 3 = ?
2. Where are the four groups of three in the problem 3 + 3 + 3 + 3?
3. What do we call this math sign: "x"?

Understand

1. What are we saying if we have (#) groups of (#)?
2. Why will using multiplication give us the answer we want?
3. What does it mean when we say we can use addition (+) or multiplication (x) ?

Apply

1. Tell me how to solve the problem in a different way.
2. Why would you choose to write the problem as multiplication instead of addition?
3. Would you be able to use multiplication to solve the following problem? Why, or why not?

   You have six bags. There are five apples in each of two bags and there are four oranges in each of the other bags. How many apples do you have, total?

Analyze

1. How are multiplication and addition similar? How are they different?
2. Explain how 6 x 5 and 5 x 6 can give you the same answer but mean different things.

Evaluate

1. Which is more important to use in problem solving: multiplication or addition?
2. How can you determine the best time to use multiplication in place of addition?

Create

1. Can you prove that using multiplication for addition works for some problems, but not all?
2. Can you create a rule for when to use multiplication in place of addition?

—Kim Swankler, Greensburg Diocese, Pennsylvania

Q–Card
Stems Associated with Questioning and Answering at All Cognitive Levels

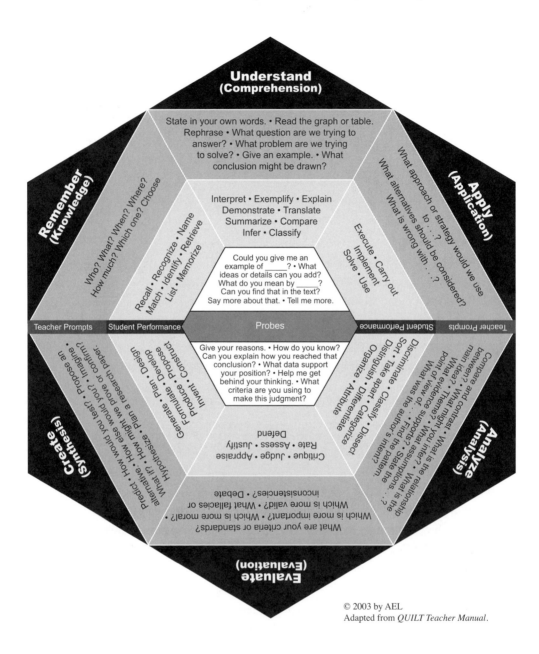

Understand (Comprehension)

State in your own words. • Read the graph or table. Rephrase • What question are we trying to answer? • What problem are we trying to solve? • Give an example. • What conclusion might be drawn?

Interpret • Exemplify • Explain Demonstrate • Translate Summarize • Compare Infer • Classify

Remember (Knowledge)

Who? What? When? Where? How much? Which one? Choose

Recall • Recognize • Name Match • Identify • Retrieve List • Memorize

Apply (Application)

What approach or strategy would we use to . . . ? What alternatives should be considered? What is wrong with . . . ?

Execute • Carry out Implement Solve • Use

Could you give me an example of _____? • What ideas or details can you add? What do you mean by _____? Can you find that in the text? Say more about that. • Tell me more.

| Teacher Prompts | Student Performance | Probes | Student Performance | Teacher Prompts |

Give your reasons. • How do you know? Can you explain how you reached that conclusion? • What data support your position? • Help me get behind your thinking. • What criteria are you using to make this judgment?

Create (Synthesis)

Predict • How would you test? • Propose an alternative. • How might we prove or confirm? Hypothesize • What if? • How else would you? • Imagine • Plan a research paper.

Generate • Plan • Design Formulate • Develop Invent • Construct Produce • Compose

Analyze

Compare and contrast • What you infer? • What is the relationship between . . . ? • What might you infer? • What is the main idea? • What evidence of . . . Theme? • What supports . . . ? • State the point of view or . . . • Find the pattern. What was the author's intent?

Discriminate • Dissect Sort • Take apart • Categorize Distinguish • Differentiate Organize • Attribute

Evaluate (Evaluation)

What are your criteria or standards? Which is more important? • Which is more moral? Which is more valid? • What fallacies or inconsistencies? • Debate

Critique • Judge • Appraise Rate • Assess • Justify Defend

The Knowledge Dimension

The knowledge dimension of the revised Bloom Taxonomy includes four categories: *factual, conceptual, procedural,* and *metacognitive.* These four levels also lie along a continuum, from concrete *(factual)* to abstract *(metacognitive).* In Chapter 6, we'll consider metacognitive knowledge in some detail as we discuss teaching students how to become more effective questioners and thinkers.

The knowledge dimension is a useful tool in helping us think about content focus, one of the four functions we associate with formulation of quality questions. The authors of the revised taxonomy define the four levels in the knowledge dimension as follows:

- *Factual knowledge* is knowledge of discrete, isolated content elements— "bits of information." It includes knowledge of terminology and knowledge of specific details and elements.

- *Conceptual knowledge* is knowledge of "more complex, organized knowledge forms." It includes knowledge of classifications and categories, principles and generalizations, and theories, models, and structures.

- *Procedural knowledge* is "knowledge of how to do something." It includes knowledge of skills and algorithms, techniques and methods, as well as knowledge of the criteria used to determine and/or justify "when to do what" within specific domains and disciplines.

- *Metacognitive knowledge* is "knowledge about cognition in general as well as awareness of and knowledge about one's own cognition." It encompasses strategic knowledge; knowledge about cognitive tasks, including contextual and conditional knowledge; and self-knowledge. (Anderson & Krathwohl, 2001, pp. 55-60)

The cognitive process dimension and the knowledge dimension are the two organizers of the Taxonomy Table (shown on page 32 of this book). Using this Taxonomy Table to classify a question requires that we first locate both the verb and the noun within the question. We can then classify the verb by reference to the cognitive process dimension and the noun by reference to the knowledge dimension. Our question then could be placed at the intersection of the two dimensions.

Employing the taxonomy as we formulate questions produces benefits for teachers and students. Teachers with whom we have worked report the value in teaching students "a language of thinking" based upon verbs associated with each of the cognitive levels and process dimensions of the revised Bloom Taxonomy. By learning this language, students are equipped to be more metacognitive—that is, to think about their own thinking. They become more comfortable responding to items on standardized tests because they have learned to recognize the kind of information processing to be embedded in correct responses.

We find the revised Bloom Taxonomy to be an invaluable tool to teachers as they structure such opportunities. However, we can offer a number of less complex alternatives, each of which distinguishes between simple recall (or remembering) and the higher-level operations.

Marzano's Taxonomy

Robert J. Marzano (1993), whose research and development focus on instructional strategies associated with student thinking and achievement, offers a two-part taxonomy composed of *recitation questions* and *construction questions*. In this schema, recitation questions are those that ask students to "simply retrieve information previously learned." For example, "What factors contributed to the stock market crash of 1929?" Construction questions, on the other hand, "require students to construct new knowledge—that not previously learned." For example, "How did the public reaction to the fall of the stock market following September 11, 2001, compare to the Crash of 1929?" Assuming this information had not been covered in class, this would be classified as a *construction question.*

Gallagher and Aschner's Taxonomy

Another well-known classification system, developed by Gallagher and Aschner (Aschner, Gallagher, Perry, & Afsar, 1961), includes three categories: *recall, convergent,* and *divergent.* In this scheme, *recall* is equivalent to the *remember* level in the cognitive process dimension of the revised Bloom Taxonomy. The other two terms do not have a one-on-one correspondence with the Bloom Taxonomy. *Convergent questions* are those that call for students to give one correct response; they call for convergent thinking—that is, as the name implies, a narrowing or focusing of the thought process. *Divergent questions,* on the other hand, allow for a number of different or alternative correct responses. In other words, there is no one right answer to a divergent question. Students are called upon to think of new and different possibilities that are justifiable, given their knowledge and understanding of the issue. In most instances, divergent questions will be the most complex of these three types and, as a result, the most difficult to conceive and formulate.

Reading Teachers' Taxonomy

Reading teachers have long used a three-part schema for talking to students about reading comprehension: *reading the lines, reading between the lines,* and *reading beyond the lines.* This classification schema can be applied to questions. If a question asks for an answer that comes from *reading the lines,* then the answer is "right there" in the text. If a questions calls for children to read *between the lines,* it asks them to think about what the text is saying—for example, to translate the author's words into their own, to analyze a character's personality, and so forth. Finally, if a question's answers are based upon *reading beyond the lines,* it asks the readers to bring their own perspectives to the text. Usually these questions are at the *Evaluate* and *Create* levels of the revised Bloom Taxonomy.

Walsh and Sattes's Taxonomy

In our research on teachers' classroom questioning practice, we devised a three-level system to use in coding teacher questions by cognitive level: *recall, use,* and *create. Recall* questions correspond to questions at the *remember* level of the cognitive process dimension of the revised Bloom Taxonomy (the *knowledge* level of the original taxonomy). *Use* includes questions at the *understand, apply,* and *analyze* levels of the revised Bloom Taxonomy, and *create* subsumes questions at the *create* and *evaluate* levels. Kindergarten teachers report success in using this simplified schema with their students. Young children can easily distinguish between questions that ask them to (1) simply recall what they have learned, (2) do something with what they have learned, and (3) use their imaginations to go beyond what they have learned or been told. Marie Rose adapted well-known myths for use in teaching her middle school students about levels of questions (see "Practice in Classifying Questions"). You might want to use a similar strategy to introduce different levels of cognitive processing to your students.

Practice in Classifying Questions

To practice using the Walsh and Sattes classification system, read each of the following three lesson summaries and classify the questions as *recall, use,* or *create.* The answers, written upside down, appear at the end of these examples.

Story 1. King Midas and the Golden Touch

Summary: King Midas finds a satyr, keeps him for a week, and then returns him to the god Dionysus. Dionysus rewards Midas by granting him a wish. King Midas wants to be able to turn things into gold by simply touching them. He realizes the harm in this when he can't eat (his food turns to gold) and when he loses his daughter, who is turned into a gold statue. He requests that this power be removed from him. When he returns home, he finds his daughter has returned to normal.

Moral: Be careful what you wish for.

Questions

1. Give examples of others who have suffered because of greediness. Your examples can be real or fictional.

2. Who grants Midas the wish?

3. Write a biopoem of King Midas.

4. Think of an alternative wish that King Midas might have requested. What unexpected outcomes might have resulted from the granting of this wish?

Story 2. The Dog and the Shadow

Summary: A dog has a large piece of meat. He sees his reflection in the water and thinks it's another dog with a bigger piece of meat. He tries to get it and loses his own meat in the process.

Moral: One may lose the substance by reaching for the shadow.

Questions

1. In your own words, tell what happened in this story.

2. How is this story like the story of King Midas? How is it different?

3. What question might you ask the dog if you were interviewing him about what happened?

4. Create another story illustrating this same moral.

Story 3. The Fox and the Grapes

Summary: A fox tries to get some grapes that are hanging over his head. He can't reach them and decides they are probably sour anyway.

Moral: People scorn what they cannot have.

Questions

1. What does it mean when someone says "That's just sour grapes"?

2. Predict what would have happened if the fox had reached the grapes.

3. Write about an event in your life when you felt the same way the fox did.

4. Why do you think the fox decided the grapes were sour?

Story 3: 1. Use 2. Create 3. Create 4. Use

Story 2: 1. Use 2. Use 3. Create 4. Create

Story 1: 1. Use 2. Recall 3. Create 4. Create

Note: These lesson summaries and questions were formulated by Marie Rose, a middle school teacher from Cabell County, West Virginia. Reprinted, with permission, from Walsh & Sattes, 2003, pp. 232-233.

A visual display or graphic is a great way to help children learn such a classification scheme. We use the visual of a three-story house to represent our three-part framework: *recall, use,* and *create*. The visual was inspired by a pithy quote from "The Poet at the Breakfast Table," an 1872 essay by American writer Oliver Wendell Holmes:

> *There are one-story intellects, two-story intellects, and three-story intellects with skylights. All fact collectors who have no aim beyond their facts are one-story men. Two-story men compare, reason, generalize, using the labor of fact collectors as their own. Three-story men idealize, imagine, predict—their best illumination comes from above the skylight.*

Imagine a permanent bulletin board in your classroom depicting this visual. What a fun and practical teaching tool this is—especially for visual learners. The three-story house further provides teachers and students with a common language for talking about thinking and questioning.

The three-story house, a fun and practical way to introduce students to different levels of cognition, is reminiscent of the work of cognitive scientists at Harvard University's Project Zero. David Perkins (1992), longtime co-director of this research center for cognitive development, offers the following three goals for education: (1) retention of knowledge; (2) understanding of knowledge, and (3) active use of knowledge (p. 5). Perkins argues that pursuit of these three goals is essential for the attainment of what he calls *generative knowledge*—knowledge that can be "put to work" in real-life situations:

Recall, Use, Create: A Visual Depiction

3rd–Create
Evaluate, Check, Coordinate, Detect, Monitor, Test, Critique, Judge, Generate, Plan, Produce, Hypothesize, Design, Construct

2nd–Use
Understand, Interpret, Exemplify, Classify, Summarize, Infer, Compare, Explain, Apply, Execute, Implement, Analyze, Differentiate, Organize, Attribute

1st–Recall
Remember, Recognize, Identify, Retrieve

Note: A participant at one of our QUILT trainings introduced us to a version of this visual, first developed by Skylight Professional Development and later adapted by Art Costa. Skylight uses a different scheme: Level 1, Gathering; Level 2, Processing; and Level 3, Applying.

"puzzling over public issues, shopping in the supermarket, deciding for whom to vote, understanding why political turmoil persists at home and abroad, dealing with an on-the-job human-relations problem and so on" (pp. 5-6).

We like to align our *recall, use,* and *create* classification system with Perkins' three goals because this schema moves considerations of classifications and levels of cognition beyond an academic exercise—it connects these considerations to the intended results we want for our students, regardless of the grade level or content area at which we teach.

Considerations in Choosing and Using a Taxonomy

We would never advocate the use of the revised Bloom Taxonomy or any other classification schema as an end in and of itself. Rather, we see these tools as means by which we teachers can help our students realize their potential as lifelong learners and citizens. Which taxonomy, or classification system, should you use?

The choice is yours. We have presented a number of well-known classification schemas but not an exhaustive listing. You may already be using another framework that is working for you and your students. In the words of the familiar adage, "If it ain't broke, don't fix it." But if you are not currently using such a tool, we encourage you to consider which classification schema best fits your instructional approach—taking into account such factors as the developmental level of your students, the content area(s) that you teach, your own personal preferences and professional strengths, and so forth.

There is no one right approach to classification. However, school faculties with whom we have worked report that schoolwide use of one system is advantageous to both teachers and students. Teachers are able to talk together about instructional objectives and questions using a common vocabulary. They are also able to develop and share questions collaboratively, a tremendous benefit, given the time-consuming nature of question formulation. Students benefit when all teachers in a school are "singing from the same song sheet." They are able to move more seamlessly from one class or grade level to the next—continually building on and enriching their metacognitive skills.

A number of caveats are in order regarding the use of Bloom's Taxonomy or any classification scheme. First, the actual cognitive level of a response is dependent upon both the context in which a question is posed and the students' experiential and knowledge background. For example, asking a student to identify an unknown substance in a science classroom requires *analysis* skills if the student has not previously confronted such a problem. If, however, the student had previously conducted such an analysis, *understanding* might be the highest cognitive level engaged.

Second, researchers have found that, on average, 50 percent of student answers to oral questions posed by their teachers do not match the cognitive level of the questions themselves (Cotton, 1988, p. 6). What can we do to remedy this dilemma? One strategy is to teach students the "language of thinking," as discussed earlier. Further, we know that some of the most important teacher questions are those that we ask in response to a student's answer—in order to get behind the student's thinking. We will examine strategies associated with such probing in Chapters 4 and 5.

Third, most questions in textbooks and teacher guides are at the lowest levels of the Bloom Taxonomy (Davis & Hunkins, 1966, p. 23; Trachtenberg, 1978, p. 117). This is largely due to the tendency of texts to "do the thinking" for students by including analyses and evaluations in the text. As a result, many text-provided questions that *look* like higher-level questions are simple remembering or recall questions. For example, consider a familiar question from American history: *What were the primary causes of the Civil War?* This question certainly could qualify as an analysis question if posed after students had read primary source materials. However, American history texts commonly provide students with a listing of the causes. In this context, the question is actually at the *remembering* or *recall* level.

Finally, many teachers assume that lower-ability students cannot answer questions at higher cognitive levels. In fact, students of all ability levels—including those receiving special education services—can think at higher levels if given adequate support and instruction. The key is to provide students with structured learning opportunities that take them through the steps associated with higher levels of cognition in a clear, sequential fashion (Bulgren, Lenz, Marquis, Schumaker, & Deshler, 2002).

Quality Questions Are Clear and Concise

Having decided on a question's instructional purpose, specific content, and cognitive level, we as teachers are finally ready to formulate our question. It helps to *write* the question; when it appears in print, flaws are easier to see. Also, you can read it a second and third time to see if the meaning is clear.

Both wording and syntax are critical to the ultimate quality of the question. Think about it. When we pose a question to students, we assume that they understand it as we mean it. But we need to consider our questions from the students' perspective:

- Do students know what the question means? Can they translate it into their own language?
- Will students have a common understanding of the kind of response the question is seeking?

If the questions we ask are clear, specific, and precise, we can answer the above concerns in the affirmative.

We need to choose our words with care. First, each word should have a clear meaning. Second, each question should include the minimum number of words necessary to convey meaning. This is particularly important when the question is to be delivered orally. Finally, the words should be appropriate to our students' age, grade, achievement level, cultural background, and so forth.

Wording and Gender

Some believe gender is another important consideration in the selection of words. John Bell, Director of the Alabama Leadership Academy, believes this merits more attention and research. As he ponders the dilemma of "saving the high school male" and helping create an awareness of the problem in today's urban schools, he wonders: Does the way the teacher words a question impact how males respond? Does the position of the question within the lesson or class period influence male engagement? Bell's investigations of these issues have convinced him that teachers (who are predominantly female) use words in their questions that may not clearly communicate to their male students.

In their book *Boys and Girls Learn Differently!*, Michael Gurian and Patricia Henley (2001) write, "Girls are generally better listeners than boys, hear more of what's said, and are more receptive to the plethora of details in a lesson or conversation. This gives them great security in the complex flow of conversation and thus less need to control conversation with dominant behavior or logical rules. Boys tend to hear less and more often ask for clear evidence to support a teacher's or other's claim. Girls seem to feel safe with less logical sequencing and more instructional meandering" (p. 46).

Syntax is equally important to forming a clear question. *Syntax* refers to the structure of the sentence and the manner in which the words are put together. Three considerations guide our thinking as we look at the syntax of questions:

1. Is the question *grammatically correct*? When we fail to consider our questions in advance, we pose questions that are not complete sentences or ask questions using run-on sentences, misplace phrases, and subject-verb disagreements.

2. Does it address one and only one issue for response; that is, is it single-barreled, *not double barreled*? Asking double-barreled questions comes from not being clear about the content focus of the question—and not having taken the time to formulate a clear question in advance of asking it. It is a common mistake to ask a question that requires more than one response—for example, "What do you think precipitated the Boston Tea Party, and were we in the right when we did that?" Which question should

students answer? The first part (the cause of the Boston Tea Party) or the second part (the rightness or wrongness of actions taken by revolutionaries)?

3. Finally, is the question stem *complete*? Does it provide students with sufficient contextual information to enable an accurate response? It is often helpful to make a statement before posing the question itself so as to make the question short enough to be understandable. For example, imagine responding to the following: "Name three or four reasons for the findings from research that teachers in K-12 education ask more than 50 percent of their questions at the recall level of the Bloom Taxonomy." By the time you hear the end of the question, you may have forgotten what was being asked. However, if the solicitation were presented as an initial statement followed by a request for a response, the listener would have more context for formulating an answer. "Research consistently finds that more than 50 percent of the questions posed by K-12 teachers are at the recall level of the Bloom Taxonomy. Give three or four reasons why this is so."

Questions for recitation and discussion are ultimately posed via the spoken word. Consequently, the acid test of a quality question is to read it aloud and assess the ease with which it is spoken. Does it feel right? Does it sound right? Is it easy to say? Is it easy to understand? If yes, the question is finally ready to leave the drawing board and be put into service in the classroom.

Quality Questions Are Seldom Asked by Chance

Without doubt, the preparation of quality questions can be time consuming and arduous; however, it is comforting to remember that a few *pivotal questions,* carefully crafted, can move a class into the heart of a lesson—and move student thinking to higher levels. If questions are one of a teacher's basic stocks-in-trade, the time invested in preparing *pivotal questions* is warranted. Once these questions are formulated and used successfully, they can and should be stockpiled for future use and shared with colleagues. A computer or card file of purposeful, significant, workable questions at all cognitive levels is potentially the most valuable resource available for teaching a particular unit.

From the asking and answering of pivotal questions, other questions emerge. Both teacher and students can pose *emerging questions* to clarify or extend understandings. Classroom questioning is a dynamic, fluid process. By asking and answering *emerging questions,* students can extend the frontiers of their learning.

When we consider all the good work that quality questions can do, we begin to see them as the "muscles" of classroom instruction. As we build these muscles, we increase their power to lift our students' learning and thinking to new heights. However, like powerful muscles, quality questions are seldom created by chance. Rather, we must craft them according to instructional purpose, content focus, desired cognitive level, and learner needs and interests.

Questions for Reflection

Formulating the Questions:
Do I plan and word key questions in advance?

*This tool for self-reflection includes reminders of
questioning behaviors associated with effective questioning.*

Questioning Behaviors	Questions for Reflection
Identify instructional purpose.	What is the purpose of my question? • Is it to reinforce knowledge, or to engage students in discussion that causes them to think at higher levels? • In what ways do the questions build group cohesiveness or involve, interest, and motivate students?
Determine content focus.	For which facts, concepts, and skills are learners accountable? • Are these facts, concepts, and skills important? • Do the questions, taken together, lead to *essential learnings* and *enduring understandings?* • Is the content aligned with district and state curricula and assessments?
Select cognitive level.	At what cognitive level are students responding? • Are students remembering, understanding, applying, analyzing, evaluating, or creating? • Are student responses at the level of the questions? • Do my questions include a variety of cognitive levels during the course of a lesson? • Do students have the prerequisite knowledge to respond correctly?
Consider wording and syntax.	Do students understand the question? Do they understand what is being asked of them? • Is the meaning clear? • Is the question specific? Is it limited to a single topic? • Is the question tightly worded? • Is the question phrased so that it can be spoken with ease?
Reflect on related beliefs.	To what extent do you and your students share the following beliefs? • Good questions help students learn. • Divergent thinking is important.

References

Anderson, L. W., & Krathwohl, D. R. (Eds.). (2001). *A taxonomy for learning, teaching, and assessing: A revision of Bloom's Taxonomy of educational objectives.* New York: Addison Wesley Longman.

Aschner, M. J., Gallagher, J. J., Perry, J. M., & Afsar, S. F. (1961). *A system for classifying thought processes in the context of classroom verbal interaction.* Urbana: University of Illinois.

Appalachia Educational Laboratory. (1994, February). *Questioning and Understanding to Improve Learning and Thinking (QUILT): The evaluation results.* A proposal to the National Diffusion Network documenting the effectiveness of the QUILT professional development program. Charleston, WV: Author. (ERIC Document Reproduction Service No. ED403230)

Barell, J. (2003). *Developing more curious minds.* Alexandria, VA: Association for Supervision and Curriculum Development.

Bellanca, J. (Ed.). (2002). *The best of SkyLight: Essential teaching tools.* Arlington Heights, IL: SkyLight Training and Publishing.

Bloom, B. S. (1987). *Taxonomy of educational objectives. Book 1: Cognitive domain.* New York: Longman.

Bulgren, J. A., Lenz, B. K., Marquis, J., Schumaker, J. B., & Deshler, D. D. (2002). *The effects of the use of the question exploration routine on student performance in secondary content classrooms* (Research Report No. 20). Lawrence: Kansas University, Institute for Academic Access. (ERIC Document Reproduction Service No. ED469289)

Caine, G., & Caine, R. N. (1994). *Making connections: Teaching and the human brain.* Menlo Park, CA: Addison-Wesley.

Christenbury, L., & Kelly, P. P. (1983). *Questioning: A path to critical thinking.* Urbana, IL: ERIC Clearinghouse on Reading and Communication Skills and the National Council of Teachers of English.

Cotton, K. (1988). *Classroom questioning* (School Improvement Research Series: Research You Can Use, Close-up #5). Portland, OR: Northwest Regional Educational Laboratory.

Davis, O. I., & Hunkins, F. P. (1966). Textbook questions: What thinking process do they foster? *Peabody Journal of Education, 43,* 285-292.

Dillon, J. T. (1983). *Teaching and the art of questioning* (Fastback 194). Bloomington, IN: Phi Delta Kappa.

Dillon, J. T. (1984). Research on questioning and discussion. *Educational Leadership, 42*(3), 50-56.

Dillon, J. T. (1988). *Questioning and teaching: A manual of practice.* New York: Teachers College Press.

Gurian, M., & Henley, P. (2001). *Boys and girls learn differently!* San Francisco: Jossey-Bass.

Hunkins, F. P. (1995). *Teaching thinking through effective questioning* (2nd ed.). Boston: Christopher-Gordon Publishers.

Jensen, E. (1996). *Brain-based learning.* Del Mar, CA: Turning Point Publishing.

Linton Professional Development Corporation. (1999). *Questioning to stimulate learning and thinking: Secondary level* (Video Journal of Education), presented by Jackie Walsh and Beth Sattes. Sandy, UT: Author.

Marzano, R. J. (1993). How classroom teachers approach the teaching of thinking. *Theory Into Practice, 32*(3), 154-160.

Mayer, R. E. (1999). *The promise of educational psychology: Learning in the content areas.* Upper Saddle River, NJ: Prentice-Hall.

McTighe, J., & Wiggins, G. (1999). *The understanding by design handbook.* Alexandria, VA: Association for Supervision and Curriculum Development.

Perkins, D. (1992). *Smart schools: From training memories to educating minds.* New York: Free Press.

Trachtenberg, D. (1974). Student thinking in text material: What cognitive skills do they tap?, *Peabody Journal of Education, 52,* 54, 57.

Walsh, J. A., & Sattes, B. D. (2003). *Questioning and understanding to improve learning and thinking: Teacher manual* (2nd ed.). Charleston, WV: AEL.

Wiggins, G., & McTighe, J. (1998). *Understanding by design.* Alexandria, VA: Association for Supervision and Curriculum Development.

Wilen, W. W. (1991). *Questioning skills for teachers: What research says to the teacher* (3rd ed.). Washington, DC: National Educational Association. (ERIC Document Reproduction Service No. ED332983)

Chapter 3:
Who Will Answer? Engaging *All* Students in Answering Questions

Focus Questions

How can we convince all students that their answers matter to us?

How can we engage all students in coming up with their own answers to each of our questions?

How can we promote equitable participation of all subgroups of students in classroom questioning?

Dull. Monotonous. Pointless. Boring. Not exciting. These were the adjectives a group of high school students used to characterize classroom questioning as they had experienced it. When asked if they knew who would answer the teacher's questions in any given class, one student responded, "Yes. You always know." Every student in the group agreed.

These student perceptions mirror the findings of research studies. For example, in a study of fourth-through eighth-grade students, researchers found that 25 percent of the students never participated in class (Sadker & Sadker, 1985). Another study, focused on secondary science classrooms, found that about 29 percent of the study's 1,245 students were completely silent, having no class interactions at all. A very small number of students (about 15 percent) dominated class interactions, averaging more than 16 interactions per class, while their almost inaudible classmates averaged fewer than four (Jones, 1990).

Target students is the designation given to the small number of students in most classrooms who answer most questions and receive a disproportionate amount of the teacher's attention. Research findings raise troubling questions about differential interaction patterns of students by gender, race, and achievement levels—with White males receiving a significantly higher proportion of classroom interactions (Tobin &

> "From an equity perspective, there is concern that a small proportion of students receive [nearly] five times more interactions than the rest of the class. The fact that teachers have greater expectations for target students raises further concern when not all students are having equal opportunities to participate in class."
>
> (Jones, 1990, p. 659)

Gallagher, 1987; Sadker & Sadker, 1994; and Wells, 2001). Equity issues are particularly relevant in this age of high-stakes accountability. Students from the subgroups that are failing to make adequate yearly progress in many schools—that is, students from low-income households, special education students, English language learners, African Americans, and Latinos—are the ones that these researchers have identified as having large numbers of nontarget students.

In *Horace's Compromise,* published in 1984, Theodore Sizer provided a portrait of "Melissa," a prototype of the unengaged, unmotivated student whom he found in American high schools. Sizer offered the following reasons for Melissa's detachment from her classes.

- Her teachers do not require her to be engaged.
- She feels no intrinsic pressure to be engaged because of the disconnect between her world and classroom curriculum.
- She is afraid; she does not want to take risks in front of her peers and teacher.
- Her goal is just to "get through" high school, and she believes the easiest path is to simply show up and go through the motions. (p. 163)

Two decades later, the high school students mentioned at the opening of this chapter seem to be offering the same reasons for student disengagement from classroom questioning. They state that "most kids don't participate because the teacher waits on the same students to answer." (Teachers do not require them to be engaged.) They say most questions "do not relate to them or their lives." (Students see no connection between their world and the classroom curriculum.) They say many students seem to feel "intimidated," or at least "uncomfortable," during classroom questioning. (They are afraid.) Further, they suggest that the primary reasons for teacher questioning are to "see if anyone is paying attention" and simply to "get through the lesson." (The students' goal is to "get through" it and take the path of least resistance.)

If this is the reality of most classrooms today, we should be asking *why?* And what can we do to change it? We must confront a number of issues if we are to answer these questions honestly and productively.

1. What do we really believe about the relationship between classroom questioning and student learning? To what extent do we believe questions are powerful tools to help every student make meaning of classroom curriculum?

2. What is the quality of the questions we ask? To what extent do we use what we know about effective questioning?

3. How do we define our role, as teacher, in the classroom learning transaction? How do we encourage our students to define their roles and responsibilities?

4. What kinds of structures do we use to get all students involved in answering and asking questions?

Beliefs and Attitudes Set the Stage

In the opening chapter, we presented our vision of what an energized, engaging classroom looks like. A key element is *shared beliefs*—those beliefs held in common by teacher, students, parents, and others in the school community. How do you react to the three beliefs listed below? How would your students respond? What would their parents say? How do you think your colleagues view these beliefs? Take a few minutes to reflect on the following belief statements from each of these perspectives.

- Good questions help students learn.
- All students can respond to all questions.
- All students' answers deserve respect.

Now think about what you are doing to demonstrate your own beliefs in each of these areas. What are the implications of your behaviors? What are the consequences?

These three belief statements are intertwined. If we truly believe that good questions help students learn, then we will formulate quality questions. We will hold all students responsible for formulating answers to all of our questions. We will ask our questions to find out what our students currently know or think about the content or issue embodied in our questions. Hence, we will demonstrate respect for all answers—right or wrong—whether the answer is the one we are seeking or a different way of viewing an issue. We will seek to get behind the student's thinking so that we can help correct misunderstandings or appreciate a different way of solving a problem.

Teacher beliefs are at the root of teacher behaviors, and teacher behaviors can have far-reaching effects on their students. A personal story illustrates the point. Will, one of Jackie's children, seemed to come into the world as an unconventional thinker. As Will went through school, his teachers took note. The contrast between two teachers' reactions to his bent illustrates the implications of teacher beliefs for practice. In a parent conference, his fourth-grade teacher said, "Will always seems to find a different way to solve problems. I can tell that he's thinking." He excelled in this classroom environment. On the other hand, a junior high school teacher told him that even though there might be merit in his answer (which did not match hers), he would have to learn to listen in class and give her the "best" answer—that is, *her* answer. He hated this class, had no respect for the teacher, and went through the motions in her classroom. Fortunately, Will is a self-confident, successful student, and he was not permanently damaged by this experience. Consider, however, the impact this teacher's attitude might have on less confident, less able students.

Many students do believe that when teachers ask questions, they are fishing for only one type of response. One high school student put it this way: "Most questions have one right answer. Even if they have more than one possible answer, teachers often have one particular answer in mind; they don't want to hear what you think." This behavior is counter to advice given by J. T. Dillon (1988), a longtime student of effective questioning. He admonishes us to "ask with interest in our students' answers"—not in hearing the right answer or the answer we're expecting, but in hearing the answer the student produces (p. 67). Otherwise, writes Dillon, the question is "lifeless," as will be the answer.

Kids will participate in classes where they feel respected, where there is mutuality of discourse (i.e., teacher and students feel they will learn something from one another—it's not a one-way street), and where they perceive a connection between the topic under discussion and what's important in their lives.

So, if we want more kids to "talk" in class, and to do so thoughtfully, and be listened to with respect by peers, we need to treat them like people who have ideas worth sharing, people whose interpretations of ideas, based on their life situations, are interesting to us.

(Fried, 2001, p. 191)

How do we demonstrate genuine interest in student answers? First and foremost, we open ourselves to authentic interest in whatever students have to say. We believe that regardless of the correctness of the student's answer, learning can follow. We deliver the question as if the answers matter to us—with expression, with care in our spoken words. Further, by scanning the room and making eye contact with multiple students, we signal our interest in their responses. Additionally, our active listening communicates volumes to students. And, as we'll explore in Chapter 4, providing time for student answers is key to eliciting responses. Note all of the ways we communicate interest in student answers prior to giving students any type of verbal feedback. Our approach affects the willingness of students to open up and engage in classroom discourse—to participate instead of vegetate.

In reality, there are many "Melissas" who have tuned out and turned off—kids who are simply going through daily motions. When and why does this happen? A number of researchers who study *student passivity*, or the tendency to avoid academic interactions, find that certain teacher behaviors encourage it, particularly in low-performing students. One of these behaviors is the failure to teach classroom communication skills—including question asking and answering—in a direct and explicit manner. Rather, students who come to school with these skills command and get more teacher attention. Over time, low-achieving students who do not arrive with these skills become more and more frustrated in their attempts to communicate, and the poor-get-poorer scenario begins (Sizer, 1984).

Thomas L. Good and colleagues (1987) assert that low-achieving students become less active classroom participants over the course of their years in school. He attributes their increased passivity to teacher behaviors: the tendency to call on low achievers less often, to provide them less wait time, to answer for them rather than try to help them answer correctly, and to praise them less often. He suggests that because low achievers have to "deal with high levels of ambiguity and risk when they respond," they learn "not to volunteer and not to answer when called upon and, possibly, to ask fewer questions and approach the teacher less often" (p. 183). In one study, he found that kindergarten males and students perceived by their teachers to be "low performing" asked more questions than females and students perceived as high achievers. As students moved through school, females asked about the same number of questions as males, but low-achieving students asked progressively fewer questions than their higher-achieving peers.

If students are less likely to participate in class interactions as they move through school, what can we do to counter this trend? First, we can practice behaviors that let students know we believe their participation is important: call on students in an equitable manner; allow wait times for all students; and provide prompts, cues, and praise without regard to ability level. Next, we can engage students in open, active discussions about shared beliefs we wish to nurture (good questions help students learn, all students can respond to all questions, all students' answers deserve respect). Finally, we can work with students to translate those beliefs into a set of norms that will help reshape their classroom behaviors.

Quality Questions Merit Student Thought

In the previous chapter we explored the four dimensions of a quality question: purposeful, well focused, at the appropriate level of cognition, and clearly worded. These are the basic ingredients of good questions. However, we can follow this recipe and still produce questions that fail to engage students if our questions are disconnected from students' experiences or do not challenge them at the appropriate level.

Too many of our questions seem irrelevant to students because the content focus has nothing to do with the students' past or present—and students are unable to see how the content relates to their futures (unless they are motivated by grades or college admission). With their teachers, they suffer through the tedium of a predictable class routine: teacher asks a question related to the text, student volunteers "the right answer," teacher nods or gives affirmative response, and teacher moves on to another question and another student volunteer. Robert L. Fried, who writes about passionate teaching and learning, calls this type of routine "the Game of School." In Fried's words, this is a "complex pattern of habits, avoidances, and defenses that creates an atmosphere in which serious learning falls victim to the drive by everyone to get through the day, the week, the year with as little hassle as possible" (2001, p. 107).

In Fried's view, most students are spectators, not players, in this game. They observe the teacher, listen to a few high-achieving participants, or simply daydream or nod off. Spectators are not involved in the kind of meaningful, thoughtful, constructivist learning that we envision. Fried argues that one of the best ways to lure students into active participation is to ask *hook questions* that are "capable of engaging students' imaginations and getting them to bring out and share expertise they already possess." These are questions for which "*all* students can offer an opinion . . . regardless of how little they know." Such questions should be asked at the beginning of a lesson, prior to the coverage of content, so that "students develop a stake in what's happening in class" and are able to connect past learnings, experiences, and attitudes to the content in the lesson. Fried's examples are imaginative:

- When dissecting frogs, we might ask: "Do humans have a right to kill animals in order to study them?"

- A class in Spanish might begin with "What will life be like when America is truly a bilingual nation?"

- In English, we could speculate: "How would our language be different if Africans had come to this continent as masters and Europeans had come as slaves?" (2001, pp. 126-127)

Think about a lesson you've recently taught. What kinds of hook questions did you use? What questions might have better captured your students' imaginations or resonated with their backgrounds?

Hook questions can lure students into a lesson. However, they will not necessarily sustain student interest over time. We need provocative essential questions to encourage our students to weave the threads of understanding over the course of a lesson or a unit. We can imagine such questions through the lens of David Perkins' idea of "'generative knowledge'—knowledge that does not just sit there but functions richly in people's lives to help them understand and deal with the world" (p. 4). Perkins and colleagues Howard Gardner and Vito Perrone developed standards for good generative topics. We think three of these standards also serve as criteria for judging the potential of a question to interest and engage students:

1. *Centrality*—Does the question focus on content that is central to the subject matter or curriculum?

2. *Accessibility*—Does the question enable students to make connections by, for example, relating new ideas to prior knowledge, finding personal examples, or looking for patterns?

3. *Richness*—Is the question robust enough to encourage a wide variety of connections and extrapolations? (Perkins, 1992, p. 93)

Consider how Christenbury's Questioning Circle, introduced in Chapter 2, might assist in generating questions that are richer and more accessible.

Mathematics is an area that can benefit greatly from the use of questions evolving from generative topics. If we want our students to truly understand the discipline of math, we might begin with the original *Standards* document published by the National Council of Teachers of Mathematics in 1989. This document focuses on the big ideas at the core of mathematics: problem solving, communication, reasoning, and connections. Ron Ritchhart, a colleague of Perkins' at Harvard's Project Zero, uses the concept of measurement to explicate how a group of first- and second-grade teachers collaborated to reinvent their approach to teaching measurement.

Through a rich dialogue, the teachers determined that "comparing" would be a more generative topic for their students than "measurement" because it seems to "capture what we do and what kids do naturally when [they] measure." One teacher observed that using comparison as the gateway to measurement would be "much more informal and natural" than his traditional approach. Another commented, "All we have to do is help focus their attention on the different attributes or characteristics that can be measured." Out of this dialogue emerged two essential questions: "How can we compare objects?" and "What does it mean to talk about *less* and *more?*" (Ritchhart, 1999, p. 464).

But what if these teachers' students had already mastered the fundamentals of measurement? Would they be engaged in thinking or talking about either of these questions? Obviously not. The conversation would be too easy or elementary for them. What about toddlers? Could they engage in a conversation on either of these questions? It would be quite the unusual two-year old! This intuitive example serves as a simple illustration of the *zone of proximal development,* a concept introduced by Lev Vygotsky, a Soviet psychologist dedicated to understanding how children develop cognitively. Although he was born in 1898, his writings were not translated into English until the late 1970s. Since then, American psychologists and educators have built on his work. Vygotsky conceptualized the zone of proximal development as that knowledge a student can learn when assisted by a mentor, either a teacher or a peer, who has mastery in the area (Oakes & Lipton, 1999).

According to Vygotsky, the role of teachers is to identify the potential area of learning for each of their students and to pose questions or provide direct instruction that will assist them in mastering content and concepts within their zones. The questions and structures serve as *scaffoldings* because they provide temporary structures around the students' learning. Vygotsky believed an important teacher role is to structure activities and groupings that keep students "stretching" within their zones. Clearly, students not working within their zones are either working with content that has already been mastered and are likely bored, or they are working beyond their readiness levels and are frustrated (Oakes & Lipton, 1999, p. 80; Wilen, 1991, pp. 178-179). If our essential questions are to capture students' imaginations, they must fall within the zone between these two extremes, the *zone of proximal development.*

New Roles and Responsibilities for Students and Teacher Are Essential

In the majority of American classrooms, the *recitation script* is dominant. Talk is directed by teacher questions, which prompt student responses, which are then evaluated by the teacher. This type of classroom discourse is also referred to as *Initiation-Response-Evaluation/Follow-up*. It has been called the "default option" to which teachers almost always return (Wells, 2001, p. 185).

We conceptualize this classroom structure as a baseball diamond where only teacher is on the pitcher's mound. Students come up to bat, one at a time. Only the target students play in this game. They answer the question directed to them (hit the ball). The teacher not only pitches, but also plays all bases and outfield positions, as he or she reacts to student hits (answers to questions). The teacher works very hard! The other students are benchwarmers, or spectators, as Fried suggested. Call to mind one class of students with whom you are familiar. How would they react to this metaphor for classroom questioning? What if you challenged them to "play" all positions over the course of a week?

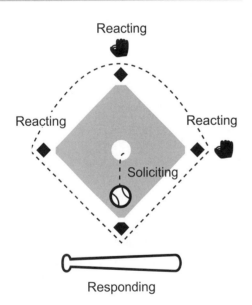

You can usually identify *target students,* or players, on the first day of school—if students are allowed to choose their own seats. They tend to sit in a position where they are most likely to receive the teacher's attention. In fact, action zone research suggests that where a student sits in the classroom determines how much interaction the student will have with the teacher (Sauer, Popp, & Isaacs, 1984). A study of 32 mathematics and social studies classes found that most verbal interaction came from students seated in the front row and center seats of other rows (see Figure 3.1). Researchers call this T-shaped area of disproportionate interactions the *action zone* and suggest that students who occupy seats in this area receive more interactions because they tend to be in the teacher's immediate view (Adams & Biddle, 1970).

What can we do, as teachers, to break up the action zone? First, we must recognize that it exists. Then we must commit to eliminating it; that is, we must have a genuine desire to make all students target students. We can begin with data collection, which might take the form of tape recording our classes and

Figure 3.1

Seating Diagram
Showing the Action Zone

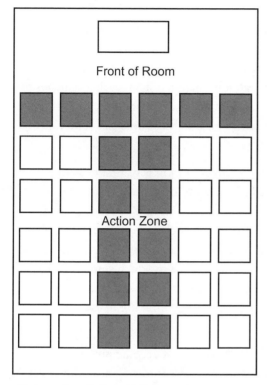

Redrawn from R. Saur, M. Popp, and
M. Isaacs, Action Zone Theory and the Hearing-
Impaired Student in the Mainstreamed Classroom,
Journal of Classroom Interaction, 19(2): 22.

listening later to identify which students were called on how many times. Or, we might ask a colleague to come into our classroom to observe for this purpose.

Once we decide to be proactive in equalizing opportunities for student responses, we can take a number of practical steps. For example:

1. Talk to students about the challenge we face to make all students target students. Give them an opportunity to discuss why their active engagement is important.

2. Be intentional in moving around the classroom. Stand in a different position every few minutes.

3. Use seating charts to position less engaged students in strategic positions. Bring them into the action zone.

4. Rotate seating periodically (e.g., weekly) so that all students have the opportunity to be at the front of the class at some point during a grading period.

5. Assess the furniture arrangement in the classroom. Does it optimize all students' view of the teacher and of one another? Many teachers cluster traditional desks into groups of three or four to facilitate cooperative groups and to create natural groupings for their classroom scans. Other teachers like the U-shaped arrangement, with desks three-deep, so that they can gain close proximity to all students.

6. Break the habit of using the recitation mode, day-in-and-day-out, by incorporating alternate response formats into your lesson planning. (The closing section of this chapter presents several for your consideration.)

Additionally, as teachers, we can ensure that every student is engaged in answering our questions. To do this, we may have to wrest control from the students themselves. Our inclination to call on volunteers to answer our questions results in student determination of who will answer. In fact, studies of target students report that the role of students in determining target (or nontarget) status is greater than that of the teacher (Jones, 1990). We've considered the role of target students in vying for and getting teacher attention as well as the tendency of low-achieving students to adopt passive classroom behaviors.

One strategy that teachers can use to counter these patterns of participation is to substitute directed questions for undirected questions during teacher-directed recitations. A *directed question* is one that a teacher directs to an individual student in a thoughtful (not random) manner. The teacher matches the question to the student by considering student interest, ability level, and so forth. *Undirected questions* are those that teachers pose to the whole class and call upon volunteers to answer.

The proper protocol for asking a directed question is to first pose the question, wait at least three to five seconds, and call upon the intended student for response. This procedure signals that all students should be ready to answer. Some teachers eliminate "hand raising" from their recitations because it implies that only those students with their hands raised are candidates for answering. Hand raising is an integral part of a classroom culture in which students believe that teacher questioning is about finding the student who has the teacher's answer to the question—not about getting behind the thinking of each student in the class.

A corresponding change in student behavior must accompany the move away from teacher deferral to volunteers for answers. Students must know that they are responsible for thinking of their answers to each and every question posed by the teacher. They must become convinced that we are interested in their answers, right or wrong, so that we can correct misunderstandings.

A corollary change is for us to "make room" for student questions as we engage in questioning sessions. The *Initiation-Response-Evaluation/Follow-up* protocol typically occurs in such a rapid-fire manner that students do not have the time or the opening to pose questions that might enhance their own and their classmates' understanding. In adopting a more thoughtful approach to whole-class questioning sessions, we encourage students to pose questions when confused or curious; we can invite them to "step onto the pitcher's mound."

As we change the norms and patterns of student answering, we achieve important instructional goals. First, we distribute questions across the entire class during a lesson and thereby encourage the engagement of all students. Second, we are able to match a given question with an individual student for the purpose of gauging the level of student understanding. In this regard, Madeline Hunter (1995) advocated the technique of "dip-sticking," asking a key question to, say, a low-achieving student to assess whether all students are ready to move ahead.

In many classrooms, teachers call on students who do not have their hands raised only when these students seem to be involved in off-task behavior. Calling upon the student, then, becomes a disciplinary tool. However, when students know that they are subject to being called upon at any time—hand raised or not, whether paying attention or not—they are more likely to maintain continual alertness and less likely to rely on their more eager classmates to do the talking.

For recitation with a whole class, then, we suggest the use of directed questions. During a class discussion, however, undirected questions are in order. Response rules should elicit student responses and permit students to answer more freely and at will. Discussions should also encourage student questions.

Further, in truly vibrant discussions, the teacher strives to become a discussant. The teacher's role is no longer to talk at every turn but to participate with students and to facilitate student thinking and talking (Dillon, 1988). Most classes need to learn new norms and ways of being together for successful discussion experiences. Most students do not arrive in classrooms with the skills and attitudes requisite for discussion—primarily because they have not experienced true discussions. Hence, teachers are well advised to provide initial instruction in norms and procedures associated with effective discussions and to use *scaffoldings* to lead students into productive discussions.

Most of us tend to use the recitation mode even when we think we're allowing student discussion. We continue to pose questions and call upon students to answer. Students continue to wait for our permission to speak and to look at and talk to us—not to one another. And, the same students tend to dominate these "wanna-be" discussions. (See Chapter 6 for a discussion of how to facilitate "true" discussions.)

Why does this recitation mode continue to dominate classrooms? Researchers have identified the following reasons:

1. It enables teachers to reaffirm their authority.
2. It allows teachers to retain most of the speaking rights.
3. It helps teachers control both the topic (through questioning) and student behavior (through the question-answer format). (Ritchhart, 1999)

We might add that in most settings, this mode is just a part of classroom culture. Students learn their roles early on. Some become players; other, spectators.

A personal story demonstrates the intricacies with which this game is played. As a ninth grader, Jackie's daughter proudly reported to her mother that she had not volunteered to answer a particular teacher's question in school that day. Her mother expressed surprise that Catherine, who was intrinsically motivated and seemingly had little need for the spotlight, considered herself a volunteer. Catherine responded, "Oh yes, I usually raise my hand *if no one else can answer* the question. I knew the answer today, but I didn't answer." When asked why, she said, "I wanted her to feel bad because she was mean to my friend. I knew she would think she hadn't taught us well if even I didn't answer." A student who was very good at the Game of School sensed that she could "punish" the teacher by withholding her response. She believed that when teacher questions were answered correctly, the teacher's authority was reaffirmed. Catherine had come to view her role as that of answering questions when others could not, but on this particular day, she stepped out of her role!

"Alternate Response Formats" Structure Patterns of Participation

Go into classrooms in almost any school on any given day and you will find the recitation mode alive and well. Teachers are standing in front of the class, or even sitting at their desks, asking questions. Students are raising their hands, or not, and answering one at a time. When certain hands go up, the other students disengage. To break out of this routine and engage all students, teachers can call on some powerful tools—what we call *alternate response formats*.

Response Formats That Aid Recitation

All of us are familiar with at least some of these strategies: *choral responses* (the class responds verbally, in unison), *signaled responses* (all students respond simultaneously by showing "thumbs up" or "thumbs down" or using some other hand signal), and *work samples* (students individually solve a problem or provide a response in writing, then show it to the teacher). These strategies are appropriate for drill and practice, checking for understanding, review, and reinforcing knowledge. They are most effective when teachers develop routines and cues to expedite their use—and then teach these to their students. For example, when using a choral response, the teacher might use a hand signal to indicate the moment for responding, thereby eliminating call-outs and assuring that all students have enough think time to formulate their own answers. As with all instructional strategies, the key to effective use is the well-planned, purposeful use of a format that matches the instructional purpose of a given lesson.

Response Formats That Aid Student–Student Interaction

Cooperative response formats afford opportunities for increased student-student interactions in the context of a teacher-directed class. One such format, known as *numbered heads together,* places students in heterogeneous teams. Teams are formed by numbering off (for example, 1–4). The teacher poses a question to the entire class, and team members in each group "put their heads together" to come to an agreement regarding an answer. After allowing time for teams to formulate their answers, the teacher calls out a number, and the student with that number on each team raises a hand. The teacher then calls on one of these students. In one research study focusing on this strategy, student failure on content-related tests was virtually eliminated (Maheady, Mallette, Harper, & Sacca, 1991, p. 31).

Think-pair-share is another simple strategy for involving all students in a teacher-directed lesson. After posing a question to the class, allow quiet time for students to consider and write their responses individually, pair students so that each student can discuss with a partner (it's helpful to have a strategy by which class members can quickly find a partner), then ask each pair to share its conclusions, observations, or viewpoints with the entire class.

Response Formats That Aid Fluid Discussion

When the object is to engage students in thinking, talking, and questioning in a fluid, conversational mode, teachers can use a variety of activities to involve all students in thinking about an issue prior to whole-class discussion. Some useful examples include the peoplegraph, synectics, data on display, interview design, fishbowl discussion, and say-it-in-a-word.

Peoplegraph. This is a more dynamic alternative to the simple pre-discussion activity of presenting the question and providing a few minutes for students to jot down their thoughts. Formulate a statement that involves a key issue and is likely to prompt divergent points of view. Then establish a continuum, an imaginary or real line in the classroom or hallway. Ask students to take a stand on the issue (literally) by physically moving to the point on a continuum—from 0 to 10, for example—that represents their level of agreement with a given statement. When all students have taken a position, provide a couple of minutes for students to share (with peers in close proximity) their reasons for taking this particular position.

Data on display. Sometimes it is helpful to generate a visual display of the opinions and beliefs of all the students in the classroom. One method for doing this is called data on display. First, develop a handout with five or six statements on an issue under study. Then get easel paper and write one of the statements across the top of each sheet. Down the left edge of each poster, create a scale from 0 to 100 percent, in 10-point increments (see Figure 3.2). Place a pad of Post-it notes at each poster. Distribute the handouts and ask students (individually) to mark the extent to which they agree with each statement, from 0 to 100 percent. Students then visit each poster and record their individual responses by placing a blank Post-it note on each chart's scale. The result is a visual display of the class's collective responses. Seeing their ideas presented this way may prompt students to speculate, draw inferences, generate hypotheses about data, and examine their own and others' assumptions. Have students reflect on the data individually, then form groups of three to five and talk about the implications of

Figure 3.2

Sample Wall Chart for Data on Display

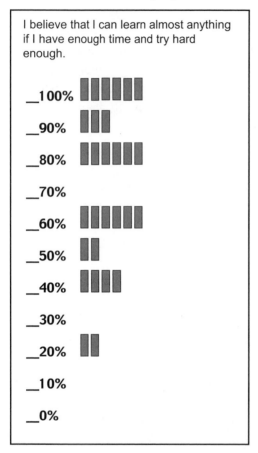

I believe that I can learn almost anything if I have enough time and try hard enough.

__100%

__90%

__80%

__70%

__60%

__50%

__40%

__30%

__20%

__10%

__0%

the data. Students are now primed for a large-group discussion. To introduce students to the process for data on display, you may wish to use the sample handout "as is" (see Figure 3.3) to engage them in thinking and talking about questions.

Synectics. Synectics is a type of structured group activity that uses metaphor or analogy to spark creative thinking and problem solving. The term has a Greek root and was coined by William J. Gordon to mean the joining together of elements that are different and seemingly unrelated. A simple form of synectics is to choose two contrasting items, such as ice cream and spaghetti. Ask students to respond individually, in writing, to the following question: "Is [topic under study] more like ice cream or spaghetti? Why?" Ask students to share their choices and reasons in small groups of three to five. Each group should select one of the metaphors (ice cream or spaghetti) and be ready to share with the larger group. The teacher might then pose a pivotal question for whole-group discussion.

A variation on this simple structure is one called four-corner synectics. Select four metaphors, post one in each corner of the room, and ask students to select the metaphor that best matches their thinking on a selected topic. (For example, "Is welfare reform more like long-distance running, mountain climbing, ice skating, or white-water rafting?") Students who select the same metaphor then meet in the corner of the room where their choice is posted. They spend five minutes or so listing reasons for their choice (e.g., why welfare reform is like white-water rafting). All four groups then share their results. Students return to their seats to continue the lesson via large- or small-group discussion or individual writing. For an example of the creative thinking this activity can promote, see Figure 3.4, Four-Corner Synectic in Action.

Interview design. One of the best tools for involving all students in asking and answering questions is called interview design. It requires advance prepara-

Figure 3.3

Thinking About Questions and Questioning
(Sample Handout for Data on Display)

I. **Directions:** Read each statement below and decide how much you agree with it. If you think it is absolutely true, circle 100 percent on the scale below the statement. If you think it is absolutely not true, circle 0 percent. For most of the statements, your opinion will be somewhere in between. Decide the extent to which you agree—from 0 percent to 100 percent—and circle that number. Use your own personal experience and opinions; there are no "right" answers in this activity.

1. When my teacher asks questions, she usually calls on the same people to answer.

    100   90   80   70   60   50   40   30   20   10   0

2. When my teacher asks questions, I almost always try to answer them to myself.

    100   90   80   70   60   50   40   30   20   10   0

3. When my teacher asks questions, she usually has one "right" answer in mind.

    100   90   80   70   60   50   40   30   20   10   0

4. My teacher's questions help me think, learn, and do well in class.

    100   90   80   70   60⌐   50   40   30   20   10   0

5. My teacher expects everyone in the class to have an answer for every question she asks.

    100   90   80   70   60   50   40   30   20   10   0

6. If I give an incorrect answer to a question, my teacher usually tries to find out why I answered as I did.

    100   90   80   70   60   50   40   30   20   10   0

II. **Directions:** When you have completed your ratings of each statement, use blank Post-it notes to mark your responses (percentages) on the wall chart for each question.

III. **Group Discussion:** After everyone in your group has added their Post-it notes to the wall charts, begin discussing the six statements and the patterns of response that have been posted by the class. As you look at the data, what questions do you have? What inferences can you make?

Figure 3.4

Four–Corner Synectic in Action
What Does Effective Classroom Questioning Look, Sound, and Feel Like?

Many times in our professional learning sessions on effective questioning, we use a four-corner synectic to get participants thinking about their vision for effective questioning. We proceed as follows.

1. First we ask participants to take three or four minutes to jot down their responses to the following prompt.

Imagine a classroom in which questioning is motivating, promoting, and supporting student learning. What would you see, hear, and feel in such a classroom? What would the teacher be doing? What would the students be doing?

2. Then we ask them to decide whether their vision of effective classroom questioning is more like (a) deep-sea fishing, (b) white-water rafting, (c) mountain climbing, or (d) scuba diving. They then get together with others who chose the same metaphor and share reasons for their selection. As a group, they brainstorm as many responses as possible to the following:

   Effective classroom questioning is like _____ *because . . . .*

Listed below are the responses provided by workshop participants in the Westmoreland Intermediate Unit, Greensburg, Pennsylvania, in November 2003.

Deep-Sea Fishing

- Throw a question out and go deeper into their thinking process
- You never know what you will "catch"
- You can chum the water with questions to engage the students ("bait the hook")
- Continue to throw out the line—continue to encourage students to continue discussion
- Letting out slack (or playing the fish)—to draw them to look at all angles of the subject
- Fisherman and the fish can be compared to teacher and students in the classroom

White-Water Rafting

- Pace is always changing; may begin fast-paced and then slow down
- Scary—trying something new; turns to exhilaration
- Lots of ups and downs
- Every trip is unique
- Members of the raft need to work together
- Quick decisions sometimes need to be made

Mountain Climbing

- Peaks and valleys
- Levels of thinking—from easier to more difficult and challenging
- Tools are essential
- Knowledge base needed
- Need a guide
- Synergy—need a team; can't do it as well alone

Scuba Diving

- Adventure/excitement
- Uncovering new things
- Element of risk but it is limited
- Lifeline to support and help
- Prior assessment of environment
- Deeper and deeper and deeper (mile deep and an inch wide)
- Quiet; time to think

tion of questions, and, in workshop settings, facing rows of chairs. But in classrooms, where it is not always convenient to rearrange furniture, students can stand in concentric circles and use a "carousel questioning" pattern to accomplish the same result. The first step is to prepare four to six questions (see sample questions, Figure 3.5). Label each question A, B, C, D, etc., and type each question on a separate sheet of paper. The following set of directions should be included on each sheet:

> Directions: Using this question, interview the person across from you. Record the responses in the space under the question and on the back of the page. You will interview several people, one at a time. Record each individual's response even if it is the same as someone else's. Record each respondent's ideas, not your interpretation. Reread the question to the person you're interviewing as needed.

Figure 3.5

Prompting Students to Think About Questions and Questioning (Sample Interview Design Questions)

1. What kinds of teacher questions motivate you to learn and do well in school?

2. What kinds of things do teachers do to encourage you to ask questions when you are confused or curious? What kinds of things prevent you from asking questions in class when you are confused or curious?

3. Why do you think most teachers ask questions in class? Think of as many reasons as you can.

4. What kinds of things can teachers do to encourage everyone in the class to pay attention and try to answer all of the questions that they ask?

Once the interview sheets are prepared, determine how many copies of each are needed. For example, suppose there are 20 students in a class, to be divided into two "interview groups" of 10 each. If five questions are prepared, four copies of each would be needed. If using the carousel arrangement, each interview group might consist of 10 students arranged in two concentric circles—5 standing in an inner circle, facing out, and 5 forming an outer circle, facing in. (The number of students in each circle should match the number of questions to be posed.) The students facing one another in pairs are each given the same interview question (A, B, C, D, or E). Each student needs a pencil, an interview sheet, and a surface to write on, such as a notebook or pad of paper.

Review the instructions printed at the top of each question. Explain that those in the inner circle will begin by posing their question to whomever they are facing. Allow one to two minutes, then call time. Announce that it is time for the respondents to become interviewers. The interviewer and respondent have the same question, which means the interviewer will now respond to the same question he or she just asked. Allow one to two minutes, then call time. Those in the outer circle should then "carousel," moving counterclockwise to their right, while those in the inner circle remain stationary. Now they are paired with students who have a different question. Each asks his originally assigned question and answers their partner's question. The paired interview process is then repeated. Continue in this manner until everyone has responded to all the questions. Note: The noise level often increases as the interviews progress and students become more comfortable and engaged.

Carousel Rotation for Interview Design

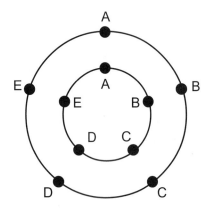

Student Positions
(First paired interview)

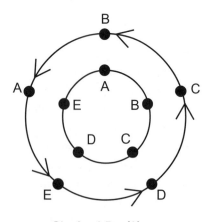

Student Positions
(Second paired interview)

The next step is analysis. After the interviewing, all four students who were *asking* the same question (A, for example) should assemble to compare responses and identify the major themes. Ask them to identify the top five themes and to record them on a flip chart beneath their question. Give each group about five to six minutes to summarize and two to six minutes to report out to the class.

Fishbowl discussion. To encourage students to engage in true discussion with one another and to listen actively to their peers, conduct a fishbowl discussion. Arrange student desks in two concentric circles, with five to seven chairs on the inside circle and the remaining chairs in the outside circle. Select four to six students to sit in the inside circle (or ask for volunteers), leaving one chair empty. Pose a question and instruct students in the inside circle to talk to one another about it. Encourage them to use what they have learned about effective questioning, such as wait time. Instruct students in the outside circle to listen and take notes so they can offer feedback later. One at a time, those in the outer circle may temporarily move to the empty chair in the fishbowl if they have questions or comments, but they must return to the outer circle as soon as they are finished. Allow 15 to 20 minutes for interactions inside the fishbowl (this will vary with age, grade level, content area, etc.).

After the discussion, debrief by asking students in the outside circle what major ideas or themes emerged, what they learned by listening to their classmates, and to what extent they think a "true discussion" occurred. Ask those inside the fishbowl how it felt to be in the fishbowl and how the experience expanded or modified their thinking.

Say-it-in-a-word. This activity is useful for engaging all students in active thinking about an issue central to a planned discussion. To begin, form a large circle that includes the teacher and all students. Pose a question that is likely to provoke some reaction from all students. Allow think time. Then ask students to think of one word that best expresses their response. Go around the circle, allowing every student to share his or her word (or to "pass").

Based on their responses, ask follow-up questions. For example, "Several of you said 'courageous.' Can you say more about why you chose this adjective?" or "Who can give me an example of how the main character was courageous?" Then encourage students to ask questions of one another and to listen to all responses.

The Power of Alternate Response Formats

Teachers can further scaffold student discussions by mind mapping major ideas offered in a discussion so that all students can follow the unfolding of the discourse. This strategy can assist less-skilled discussants in understanding the course of the conversation and can motivate more visual learners to contribute as they see the "web of talk" develop. Some might argue that these kinds of supports interfere with free-flowing discussion. But not all students arrive in classrooms with the skills requisite to thinking and talking about an assigned issue, and these supports can help them. As a teacher moves a class through a school year, she can drop scaffolds as students become more skilled and secure in their ability to function in a discussion environment.

Figure 3.6, Alternate Response Formats, lists a variety of "scaffolds" for eliciting student responses, together with instructional purposes for each. Selecting an appropriate response format to maximize the engagement of all students is a key part of lesson planning. When we fail to think through this dimension of the questioning process, we too often default to the pattern of calling on one student at a time—usually a volunteer.

Teacher instructional decisions regarding question presentation are important determinants of student participation. By reflecting on current response patterns in one's classroom, most teachers can identify ways to increase opportunities for all students to participate in answering. At the core of this issue is being intentional in deciding (1) how to pose questions, (2) who will answer, and (3) how they will answer—rather than allowing a questioning episode to unfold willy-nilly.

Figure 3.6

Alternate Response Formats

Response Strategy	Instructional Purposes
1. Choral Responses	Affording practice or reinforcement that will assist students in simple recall
2. Signaled Answers	Checking to determine if students remember or recall facts or concepts
3. Work Samples	(a) Checking to determine if students remember, understand, or can apply information; (b) offering opportunities for individual practice
4. Numbered Heads Together	(a) Providing opportunities for mastery via peer teaching; (b) holding students accountable in a cooperative learning activity, e.g., jigsaw; (c) reviewing concepts prior to testing; (d) activating prior knowledge and experience at the beginning of a new lesson or unit
5. Think-Pair-Share	(a) Affording students time to "get their thoughts together" prior to the beginning of a class discussion or a writing assignment; (b) activating prior knowledge at the beginning of a lesson; (c) reviewing
6. Peoplegraph	(a) Getting students to think about core (essential) concepts at the beginning of a unit of study; (b) engaging students in active thinking prior to discussion or written assignment
7. Synectics	(a) Developing deeper insight into a concept or topic by considering it from a different perspective; (b) promoting divergent thinking and respect for diverse points of view
8. Data on Display	(a) Providing practice with data analysis, hypothesizing, inferencing, and speculation; (b) examining assumptions
9. Interview Design	(a) Encouraging students to respect diverse points of view; (b) promoting active listening and note taking; (c) providing a structure in which *every* student answers every question; (d) affording practice in summarizing
10. Fishbowl Discussion	(a) Affording practice in active listening and note taking; (b) providing opportunities to practice discussion skills and receive feedback in a safe environment
11. Say-It-In-a-Word	(a) Activating thinking and decision-making skills; (b) promoting active listening; (c) leveling the playing field by assuring that every student has the same opportunity for initial response

Questions for Reflection
Presenting the Questions:
Do I plan to engage all students in answering?

This tool for self-reflection includes reminders of questioning behaviors that engage all students in answering.

Questioning Behaviors	Questions for Reflection
Indicate response format.	How do students respond? • Do I select response formats that match my instructional purpose? • Do students respond in writing, orally, or both? • Do I use a variety of formats? • Have I taught my students the rules and procedures for participating in each response format?
Ask the question.	Do students attend to questions? • Do all students actively listen to questions? • Do all students appear to understand questions?
Select the respondent(s).	To which student(s) do I direct questions? • Are all students on continuous alert? • Do I provide all students with equal opportunities to respond? • Do I give high-achieving and low-achieving students an equal chance to answer equally difficult questions? • Are my questions directed or undirected? • When do I call upon a student to answer—before or after posing the question?
Reflect on related beliefs.	To what extent do you and your students share the following beliefs? • All students can respond to all questions. • All students can think and reason—beyond rote memory.

References

Adams, R., & Biddle, B. (1970). *Realities of teaching*. New York: Holt, Rinehart & Winston.

Dillon, J. T. (1988). *Questioning and teaching: A manual of practice*. New York: Teachers College Press.

Fried, R. L. (1995). *The passionate teacher: A practical guide*. Boston: Beacon Press.

Fried, R. L. (2001). *The passionate learner: How teachers and parents can help children reclaim the joy of discovery*. Boston: Beacon Press.

Good, T. L., Slavings, R. L., Harel, K. H., & Emerson, H. (1987). Student passivity: A study of question asking in K-12 classrooms. *Sociology of Education, 60,* 181-199.

Hunter, M. (1995). *Mastery teaching* (rev.). Thousand Oaks, CA: Corwin Press.

Jones, M. G. (1990). Action zone theory, target students and science classroom interactions. *Journal of Research in Science Teaching, 27*(8), 651-660.

Maheady, L., Mallette, B., Harper, G. F., & Sacca, K. (1991). Heads together: A peer-mediated option for improving the academic achievement of heterogeneous learning groups. *Remedial and Special Education, 12*(2), 25-33.

National Council of Teachers of Mathematics (NCTM). (1989). *Curriculum and evaluation standards for school mathematics*. Reston, VA: Author.

Oakes, J., & Lipton, M. (1999). *Teaching to change the world*. Boston: McGraw-Hill College.

Perkins, D. (1992). *Smart schools: From training memories to educating minds*. San Francisco: Jossey-Bass.

Ritchhart, R. (1999). Generative topics: Building a curriculum around bit ideas. *Teaching Children Mathematics, 5*(8), 462-468.

Sadker, D., & Sadker, M. (1985). Is the OK classroom OK? *Phi Delta Kappan, 66*(5), 358-361.

Sadker, M., & Sadker, D. (1994). *Failing at fairness: How America's schools cheat girls*. New York: Macmillan.

Sauer, R., Popp, M., & Isaacs, M. (1984). Action zone theory and the hearing-impaired student in the mainstreamed classroom. *Journal of Classroom Instruction, 19*(92), 21-25.

Sizer, T. R. (1984). *Horace's compromise: The dilemma of the American high school.* Boston: Houghton Mifflin Company.

Tobin, K., & Gallagher, J. (1987). Target students in the science classroom. *Journal of Research in Science Teaching, 24*(1), 61-75.

Wells, G. (2001). The development of a community of inquirers. In G. Wells (Ed.), *Action, talk, and text: Learning and teaching through inquiry* (pp. 1-24). New York: Teachers College Press.

Wilen, W. W. (1991). *Questioning skill for teachers: What research says to the teacher* (3rd ed.). Washington, DC: National Education Association. (ERIC Document Reproduction Service No. ED332983).

Wilkinson, L., & Spinelli, F. (1982). Conclusion: Applications for education. In L. Wilkinson (Ed.), *Communicating in the classroom* (pp. 332-337). New York: Academic Press.

Chapter 4:
How Do Students Make Connections? Prompting to Promote Thinking

Focus Questions

How do teacher prompts promote student thinking and enhance student learning?

How does the use of Wait Times 1 and 2 benefit students and teachers?

How can teacher probing assist students in surfacing and clarifying misunderstandings and in developing correct understandings?

A second-grade student was struggling to understand a new concept. His teacher provided extended wait time and then began gentle prompting. The student finally offered an incorrect answer. The teacher stayed with him, asking additional questions in an attempt to get behind his thinking. The other students were quiet and very respectful as the teacher continued to interact with this child. Finally, after what seemed like an eternity—but was actually less than a minute—a light went on in the student's eyes, a smile, and then a correct response, followed by this sweet statement: "Thank you, Mrs. Castleberry, for helping me understand."

Joette Castleberry, a teacher in Montgomery, Alabama, shared this story four years after she began assessing and fine-tuning the questioning processes in her classroom. She reflected on this special classroom moment and said: "I would never have persevered with one student in such a manner prior to my training in effective questioning. And this was a difficult behavior for me to master. But I now believe that this is one of the most important ways a teacher can support students' learning."

If we truly believe that "all students can respond to all questions," then we consciously work to do at least three things to promote this end. First, we prepare and pose quality questions—ones that engage student thinking, are relevant and meaningful to students, and are worth answering. Second, we select response formats that engage all students in thinking about and answering our questions. Finally, as the example from Joette's classroom illustrates, we provide appropriate prompts so that students who respond have the opportunity to give full and complete answers, uncovering misunderstandings along the way.

Throughout this chapter, we consider the process of answering and highlight teacher actions that can assist students in giving complete responses. Some of these actions include using silence at strategic times to give students time to think through a response; using overt, verbal cues and prompts; and probing to help students explain their thinking or uncover incorrect reasoning.

Prompting full and complete answers takes Dillon's adage, "Listen with interest in the *student's* answer," to its logical conclusion. It requires teachers to give up the habit of rushing from question to question—and sometimes from student to student—looking for the answer they had in mind when they asked the question—the "one right answer." Indeed, the need to prompt and probe comes from a desire to fully understand a student's thinking. Consider this example from Kim Swankler's second-grade classroom in Greensburg, Pennsylvania:

> Most questions that teachers ask have one right answer. Even if the questions have more than one possible answer, teachers usually have just one particular answer in mind. They don't want to hear what you think; they just want to hear their answer.
>
> —High School Senior

We were working with manipulatives, and one of the students had written a multiplication problem on the board: 2 x 8=16. I asked students to signal with a "thumbs up" if they agreed with the answer. Then I called on one of them, David, to explain the problem so that I could see if he understood. David went up to the board but wasn't able to explain it. It would have been easy for me to interrupt and give him the answer, or to call on someone else to give the answer. But I let David take responsibility. After he thought about it a while, he asked the boy who first created the problem to come and help him. Neither one could explain what they were doing. So they asked a third boy to come up. This boy explained that it was two groups of 8. But David still didn't seem to get it. Finally, I heard him say, "one group of 8 and one group of 7," and I realized that he had miscounted the manipulatives. He couldn't see how it could be two groups of eight because he thought he was seeing a group of 8 and a group of 7. Had I not stayed with him, neither he nor I would have understood the error that was preventing him from explaining the problem. This whole exchange took about 10 minutes. The class stayed engaged because they knew that he might call on them to help. Those who understood were eager to help him; those who didn't understand were eager to hear his explanation once he figured it out.

Many of us would have sighed with relief when the first boy wrote the correct answer on the board. We would have affirmed it as correct and moved on to the next problem. But Kim opted to see if her students truly understood the concept of multiplication; she was interested in their learning the process, not just getting the right answer. She has a simple strategy that holds students responsible and accountable. "In my class, if students are stuck, they can ask for help. David did that. But sometimes, when I see a student struggling, I might ask, 'Do you want to ask for help?' and the student will say 'no' because he wants to work it out for himself. They know they always have that option."

What lessons might students learn from the experience of their teacher treating an incorrect answer with respect and providing time and support for them to come to a complete and correct understanding? What is learned in classes where teachers prompt student thinking and treat student answers with respect and care? We submit that students are learning important life lessons:

- Respect for others' ways of thinking is desirable.
- Patience—with oneself and with others—can and should be cultivated.
- The process of answering (and thinking) is as important as the answer itself.
- Thinking takes time.
- It's okay to ask for help.
- Incorrect answers will be treated with respect; there are no "stupid answers" in this class.
- Every student can think and can answer every question.
- It's my **response ability** to come up with correct and complete answers; I am accountable; no one is letting me "off the hook."

Answering As a Process

Answers to classroom questions are often viewed as products, but answering is (at least) a five-step process: (1) listen to the question, (2) understand what is being asked for, (3) answer to self, (4) answer out loud, and, sometimes, (5) rethink and revise the answer. These steps can be visualized as the children's game of hopscotch.

The first step in the process is that students *listen* as the question is asked. If students are not paying attention when the question is posed, they will not be able to answer correctly. Indeed, to what extent does failure at this first step account for some of the "wrong answers" that we hear in school?

We often overlook the necessity of the second step—to *understand* the question. Students must interpret not only the meaning of the question but the

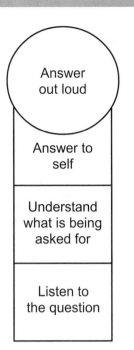

Answer
out loud

Answer to
self

Understand
what is being
asked for

Listen to
the question

Adapted from Meredith Gall (1984)

level of thinking called for in a response. This step takes different students different amounts of time. Students who are literal may hear a question and not grasp its subtlety or nuance. Students from a cultural background different from the teacher's may struggle with the vocabulary, grammatical construction, and the teacher's pattern of speech. Certainly for English language learners, this step will involve more time. These students have to translate the question into their home language before they can begin to make meaning of it. Having questions that are clear and concise—that is, having given thought to the wording and syntax—is one way to minimize difficulty with this step of the process.

The first two steps require listening and interpreting. The third step, *answer to self,* is the beginning of the formulation of a response. This is the step in which the student does or doesn't "find" an answer—be it right or wrong. The student may have heard the question and interpreted it correctly, but now she has to think of an answer before she can put it into words. Mary Budd Rowe (1986) likens the process of answering to that of finding something stored in a warehouse. The question is loaded onto the freight elevator on the first floor. The elevator goes to the appropriate level (which takes time), and then the challenge is to discover in which "bin" (or area of the brain) the answer is stored. When it is finally located, the answer (or thought) is loaded onto the elevator (from the brain) and taken to the first floor (to the mouth) where it can be unloaded (or spoken).

This fourth step—*answer out loud*—is where teachers usually focus the most attention. Typically only one student in a classroom gets to perform this fourth step, during which the silent thoughts (generated in Step 3) become expressed and clarified. Because it is through speaking our ideas aloud that we come to understand them more clearly, using cooperative response formats (as suggested in Chapter 3) allows more students the opportunity to engage in this step of the process.

Particularly for questions that are at higher cognitive levels, the process of answering continues beyond the initial response. In Step 5, students rethink and *revise their answers* based on other students' answers, their own thinking about the answer, and the teacher's reaction and feedback.

Wait Time: The "Miracle" Pause

When we consider answering as a multistep process, as described above, it is apparent that *it takes time*. How much? This depends on the difficulty of the question and the way a student thinks and attends. And students will need differing kinds of assistance along the way. Interestingly, one way to help students—and probably the single most effective thing we can do to assist thinking—is to do nothing. Simply put, to be quiet. To intentionally and systematically provide ample time for students to think—without our talking, prompting, repeating the question, or otherwise speaking.

Mary Budd Rowe (1986), formerly a science educator at the University of Florida, discovered the value of silence as she was conducting research about science instruction in K-12 classrooms. As she listened to hundreds of audiotapes of classroom interactions, she noticed that very few student questions were posed. Indeed, she came to realize that when students spoke at all, they spoke only briefly and they spoke in answers. Remarkably, Rowe found only three classrooms where this pattern was different—where students asked questions as well as answered them. When she listened again to these tapes, she identified the signal difference. In these three classrooms—and in none of the others that she listened to—teachers occasionally stopped talking; there were periodic and brief moments of silence.

Rowe named these moments "wait time." She identified two important junctures for the silence: (1) Wait Time 1—after asking a question, before designating a student to answer; and (2) Wait Time 2—after a student responds, before the teacher reacts or comments. Rowe and others, in subsequent studies, have found that most teachers typically wait less than one second at both of these points. Teachers allow even less time for students whom they perceive to be low performing (Stahl, 1994). In Chapter 1, we looked at possible reasons why teachers don't wait. One important reason is that teachers don't want to embarrass students. Mistakenly, many of us have gotten into the habit of moving quickly—not recognizing the potential value of slowing down to encourage thinking.

Researchers have discovered that teachers who extend wait times to three to five seconds open up exciting possibilities for their students and themselves. During the decades following Rowe's discovery of wait times, numerous researchers have validated the importance of this phenomenon within and beyond science classrooms. In fact, researchers report the value of wait time in myriad settings, from early childhood learning through higher education. Research studies have found the following kinds of benefits to students (see Rowe, 1986) when teachers use wait times of three to five seconds:

- **Students give longer responses.** In most classrooms, where wait time is less than one second, student answers are brief phrases; it is unusual for a student to expand or explain. But when wait time increases, so do student answers—by as much as 300 to 700 percent! Students tend to elaborate on their answers, particularly with the use of Wait Time 2, and their answers are more complex.

The Power of Wait Time 2

In my third-grade class, I'm reading aloud a book at the seventh-grade level to increase reading enjoyment and vocabulary comprehension. In one passage, the author writes that a wealthy woman "pulled in her skirts" when a poor orphan boy passed by her. You definitely had to "read between the lines" to get the meaning, and I wondered how much the children were able to pick up the meaning and develop an inference about the author's intent. I asked, "How do you think this woman felt about the kids?" And one little boy said, "She didn't like the little boy." When I asked him why, he said, "I could tell she didn't like the little boy because she pulled her skirt away when he passed by. That's because she didn't want to get dirty from his dirty clothes." And then I waited, and the boy continued, "I don't think that she was very nice. It's not a very nice way to think because we are all equal." Wow! From a third grader! These are not the kinds of answers I have gotten before from my classes—these are much more thoughtful answers, at deeper levels.

—Nancy Abramovic, third-grade teacher, Pennsylvania

- **Students give evidence for their ideas and conclusions.** When teachers use Wait Time 2 (pause after a student answer), they notice that student talk is filled with short pauses. Students are thinking as they speak, and rethinking. When teachers allow students to complete their thoughts (by using the three- to five-second wait time), students more often give evidence to support their answers. Without the extended pause, this happens only rarely.

- **Students speculate and hypothesize.** Intentionally inserting a pause before reacting to a student answer also allows students to reflect on what they have said, to rethink an answer. They are more likely to pose hypotheses and speculations about the topic under study.

Teachers say . . .
It's definitely helping my students think at higher levels. When you give the kids a chance to speak and give them enough wait time, you will be amazed at what they say to you!

- **Students ask more questions.** As we said earlier, in most classrooms—where Wait Times 1 and 2 are under one second—students speak only in answers. But when a short silence is inserted, they may be prompted to ask a question following another student's response. They may begin to question their own answers. These student questions are the mark of real learning, and we will investigate them further in Chapter 6.

- **Students talk more to other students.** In a standard recitation format, the teacher is the center of every interaction. He asks the questions and reacts to student answers. But in a classroom where the teacher intentionally pauses, students begin to listen and respond more to one another.

- **There are fewer "I don't knows."** Rowe reports that students give no answer or respond "I don't know" as much as 30 percent of the time in classrooms where wait time is short (1986, p. 45). Wait Time 1 is especially helpful in reducing these kinds of nonresponses because more students have sufficient time to develop an answer (Step 3 of the answering process). When they don't have an answer—even after they are given sufficient time—teachers can establish the option of "I pass." Rowe found that students who could "pass" were more apt to re-enter a discussion later than were students who, without adequate wait time, answered, "I don't know."

- **Discipline improves.** Most teachers resist using wait time because they worry that they will "lose students" when they move at a slower pace. Actually, it is constant, fast-paced questioning that seems to create discipline problems and inattentiveness. In studies of classrooms and in self-reports, teachers who use wait times of three to five seconds tend to have students who are more engaged with the lesson.

- **More students participate in responding.** In classrooms where wait times are used, more and varied students respond to questions. This is illustrated by the experience of a teacher who asked her class why they liked her new approach to questioning. One little girl, so shy and reserved that she had never spoken aloud to the whole class before wait time, answered, "Because everybody gets to speak." A boy, whom the teacher acknowledged to be very low performing, added, "I like it because I get to speak, too." This teacher continued her reflection, "Think of it! I've stopped rushing through the content—to try to cover it all—and this little girl appreciates it because she gets to speak! I can't believe I never knew about the value of slowing down before."

- **Students answer with more confidence.** When teachers consistently use Wait Times 1 and 2, students learn to evaluate their own responses; they become less dependent on the teacher to judge the rightness or wrongness of their answers. They less often answer a question with a tentative response. Rowe (1986) found that students with background experience in classes using wait time were able to defend their own conclusions—in the face of an expert disagreeing with them—with more persistence than the students who came from classes where no wait time had been used.

- **Achievement improves on cognitively complex test items.** Several research studies have found a correlation between the use of three- to five-second wait times and students' responses being more cognitively complex. This seems to carry over to written tests as well, as Tobin (1987) and others have found student performance to increase on cognitively complex assessments.

When teachers begin to use wait times systematically, benefits are reported not only for their students, but for the teacher as well:

- **Teacher responses are more thoughtful.** Wait time allows teachers to respond to students in a manner that keeps the conversation continuous and focused. Wait Time 2 gives teachers adequate time to create a probe or a prompt that will help a student elaborate, when appropriate. It also gives teachers time to think of feedback that will be helpful to the student.

- **Teachers ask fewer questions—and questions of higher cognitive levels.** Research findings indicate that the degree of improvement resulting from increases in both wait time and higher cognitive questions is greater than an increase in either of these variables by itself. Indeed those who have examined the relationship between these factors tell us that, in a sense, they "cause" one another. That is, the more complex mental operations required by higher cognitive questions call for—and are often found to produce—longer wait times. And increases in wait time seem to result in teachers and students carrying out recitations at higher cognitive levels (Cotton, 1988).

  Additionally, there is a correlation between use of wait time and the level of the question (Barnette, 1995). Because student responses are longer and more complex, teachers ask fewer questions. With more time to think about them, teachers tend to ask questions that are of higher quality.

- **Teachers expect more from previously nonparticipating students.** It's not uncommon to hear teachers say, after they begin using wait times, "I never would have expected an answer like that from Robert." Their expectations for students—particularly low-performing students—increase as more students participate and contribute significant answers.

The findings of the effectiveness of wait time are consistent and positive. In the words of David Berliner (reported in Swift, Gooding, & Swift, 1988), "If we were medical researchers, we would say these are miracle findings. We can cure classroom ills with no contraindications."

Others suggest additional points in time when silence is important. Robert Stahl (1994) identifies eight points in classroom discourse where silence enhances instructional objectives. He prefers to use the term *think time* rather than *wait time* because it better describes the purpose of the pause. He defines think time as "a distinct period of uninterrupted silence by the teacher and all students so that they both can complete appropriate information processing tasks, feelings, oral response, and actions" (p. 1).

Swift identified a third category, Wait Time 3—the time between the end of one student answer and another student's comment, reaction, or question. Whereas Rowe's Wait Time 2 referred to student-to-teacher pausing, Swift's Wait Time 3 applies to student-to-student interactions. We prefer to think of these two together and define Wait Time 2 as the amount of time between the end of one student's answer and the beginning of speaking by someone else—either the teacher or another student. In this way, we bring students "into the game" of wait time.

We believe it is critically important to help students understand the reason and value of wait time, commit to using it intentionally, and help monitor its use. As we suggested in Chapter 1, when we introduce classroom norms to our students, it helps to talk about them. Two of those norms—"We all need time to think before speaking" and "We all need time to think out loud and complete our thoughts"—refer directly to Wait Times 1 and 2. We like to say, "You can't do wait time *to* students; you have to do it *with* them."

Because the introduction of wait times changes a classroom fairly dramatically, it is important to spend time

Poster 1

What Teachers Often Do	What I Would Like
Teachers usually ask most of the questions.	I would like students to ask more questions.
Teachers usually don't wait after asking a question to give everybody time to think.	I want to be silent for a little while after I ask some questions so we have time to think.
After a student gives an answer, teachers usually start talking right away.	Sometimes I want to be silent after a student talks so we can think about what we hear.
Teachers are usually the ones students talk to during lessons.	I want students to ask questions and make comments to each other, instead of just me.

talking with students about it and helping them assess the merits. Many teachers who have participated in our workshops on effective questioning have found it necessary to provide students with visual or verbal cues to signal wait times. As the new behavior is being established, some teachers remind their students of wait-time norms at the beginning of a questioning episode. They might say, for example, "Now we're going to try to practice some of our effective questioning behaviors. After I ask a question, what do I want you to do?" After getting a response such as "You want us to wait," the teacher then might ask, "And why do I want you to do that?" We heard one student say, in response to this question, "Well, it takes all of us different amounts of times. We all learn differently—and process information differently. So this gives everyone time to think of an answer." Pretty sophisticated thinking for a middle school student!

Some teachers have created posters they can point to during a questioning interaction to remind students to use wait times. The samples provided here were created by Julie Porath, an elementary school teacher in Montgomery, Alabama. Other teachers use hand signals. For example, they might ask the question, raise their finger to their lips (indicating silence), count to three, and then signal with a raised hand that it's time to answer. Another hand signal that

Poster 2

Steps for
Wait Time 1

What to Do
After the Teacher Asks a Question

1. Listen carefully to the question.

2. Think of the answer yourself.

3. Remember there will be silent time for thinking.

4. Instead of raising your hand, wait to be called on.

5. Be ready to answer in a public speaking voice.

6. If you're not called on, listen carefully to your classmate's answer and think about it.

Poster 3

Steps for
Wait Time 2

What to Do
After a Student Talks

1. Remember that silent time gives us all time to think.

2. If it wasn't your turn to talk, think about what your classmate said.

3. Decide if you agree or disagree, and the reasons why.

4. Be ready to "piggyback" or add comments to what you've heard.

5. Be prepared to use your public speaking voice when it is your turn to talk.

6. Be respectful of your classmates.

Posters created by Julie Porath and reprinted, with permission, from the *QUILT Teacher Manual* (Walsh & Sattes, 2003).

is effective is to ask the question, raise the hand as a stop sign—using the fingers to count to three (or five)—and then turn the hand in an open gesture to show that it's time to respond.

To be successful in implementing wait times, teachers need cues to help *themselves* remember. One way to do this is to ask the question, then take three slow steps before calling on a student. Another way is to ask the question and, with fingers held behind the back, count "one thousand and one, one thousand and two, one thousand and three." Our personal experience has been that very often, when you reach one thousand and five—thinking, "No one is going to answer this question!"—one student volunteers a response and others follow suit.

Wait Time 2 is the more difficult to remember and use consistently. We teachers are so used to commenting immediately on a student response that it is hard to establish the habit of pausing. It becomes easier as we keep in mind that we are listening to know what *students think,* instead of listening for *our answers.* We must acknowledge, however, that it is never really natural or simple; it takes work, persistence, and patience.

Wait time seemed like a simple thing—something we all know about. But for the most part, teachers were used to asking a question and then, if they didn't get a response right away, they would ask a leading question that unknowingly gave students the answer. Wait time gives students time to think—which they need, if the questions are complex. This wasn't easy for our teachers; they were uncomfortable with it because wait time is a concept that needs feedback and practice. But now our teachers have begun to understand there is a relationship between complex questions and the use of wait time—kids require it in order to think through their answers.

—Stuart Greenberg, Deputy Director for the Eastern Regional
Reading First Technical Assistance Center, Florida

Other Ways to Encourage the Answering Process

Teachers communicate their expectation that students will respond correctly by providing students with adequate time to move through each of the five steps of answering, then offering verbal prompts if necessary. These teacher actions send a message to students: "I expect each of you to respond when called upon. The important thing is *your* response, not *my* answer." As we think about ways to prompt student thinking, we need to consider all five steps of the process of answering—listen to the question, understand the question, answer to self, answer out loud, and revise the answer. The appropriate form of teacher assistance depends on which step of the process is giving the student difficulty.

Often, we assume that when a student doesn't answer, it's because he doesn't know the answer. But students may be having trouble at any one of the steps in the process.

Failure to complete the first step *(listen to the question)* may result in a student asking, "Could you repeat the question?" Students who are less sure of themselves may be reluctant to ask the teacher—or to admit that they weren't listening. If the teacher has reason to suspect that the student didn't hear the question, she may simply repeat the question—once she is assured of the student's attention. This may be a necessary step for students who have difficulty focusing or attending, until they learn to attend when appropriate.

For example, Beth has a son who had difficulty attending to questions when he was young. She would often reach out and touch his chin, until eye contact was established, before she would pose a question. When she failed to do that, she would nearly always have to repeat the question two or three times before he attended to it. The teacher may find it helpful to provide overt clues to students, such as holding aloft a poster-board question mark and giving a verbal cue: "I'm going to ask a question. Are you ready?" Or, we can simply write focus questions on the board, or project them via an overhead or LCD projector. Alternatively, we may ask a peer to repeat the question or directly ask the student, "Would you like me to repeat the question?"

If a teacher thinks the student is stumbling at the second step of the process *(understand the question),* he or she may simply pause to allow the student time to work out the interpretation on his own. Each of us requires a different amount of time to accomplish this "translation." If the student seems to be struggling to understand, a simple prompt might be offered: "Could you say the question in your own words?" or "Maria, tell me what you think the question is asking." It may be important to rephrase the question in different words that are more closely related to the students' background and knowledge. Rarely do students admit that they don't understand the question or that they need clarification ("Do you mean . . . ?"). The teacher may see it as criticism, so it involves a certain amount of risk to the student.

> It has been said that a question, well-worded, provides two-thirds of the answer.
> —Francis P. Hunkins
> (1995, p. 39)

If the question includes "thinking words" that are unfamiliar to the student, the teacher might need to help interpret the question: "When I ask you to *generalize,* I'm asking you to look across all the examples and see if you can identify a trend or some way in which they are all similar." Until students become familiar with these words and understand their meanings, teachers may opt to provide this explanation before the question is posed. Classroom posters or other visual cues can also be helpful, as suggested in Chapter 2.

I made a poster for my classroom on the Bloom Taxonomy. I used third-grade terms and explained them to my students. I shared with them that I was learning to be a better questioner. Now before I ask a question, I'll say to them, "This is going to be an analysis question." We look at the chart, I explain in easy terms what an analysis question is, and then I ask the question and they answer it. We refer to the chart all the time.

Many students need assistance at Step 3 *(finding the answer)*. Time is an important assist at this step. But as students "rummage around" for the answer, they may be at a loss to know where to look. When this happens, we need to assist the student by helping him find the requisite facts and understandings from memory, to "know in which storage area to look." Cues and clues are overt prompts we can use when students give blank looks or respond by saying, "I don't know" or "I don't remember."

Cueing. Cues are words or symbols that can help a student respond to a given question. When cueing, a teacher may remind students of past or related learnings that trigger the memory or spark the cognitive processes required for the response. Or, the teacher may ask students to draw from personal experience—from what they *already* know—to move toward a correct response. The teacher could refer to the context or the class in which the knowledge was first introduced (e.g., "Remember on Monday when we were discussing . . . ?" "We saw an example of this when we visited the bakery." "Yesterday we talked about the first step in addition and we did it on the board. Can you remember what we did first?"). Cues might also be associated with a visual reminder (a map, picture, transparency, video, graphic organizer, etc.). Effective cues might reference related facts or concepts (e.g., "The president heads this branch of government." "Foreshadowing predicts what will happen. Can you remember anything in the first chapter that foreshadowed the events in Chapter 3?"). Mnemonics are another way to help a student connect to some memorized content.

Clueing. Closely related to cues are clues, which are more overt reminders. The teacher may provide the student with a "starter," that is, a key word, a beginning sound, first name, sounds like, or some other verbal or nonverbal clue. Even more direct, the teacher may point

We struggle with students wanting us to answer questions. They are adept at "waiting us out." We've taught them, over time, that if they don't answer, we will. It's hard. A lot of teachers are impatient. I have to watch myself because I know the answer, and I want to give it—but I have pretty much broken myself of that habit.

—Bob Holbert, 12th-grade social studies teacher, Louisville, Georgia to the correct country on the map and ask the student to read the name. Or, the teacher may share a related bit of knowledge as a catalyst for evoking the correct response. Many teachers use the strategy of reviewing the information given to date and asking additional simple questions that lead the student to the answer of the original question. Many strategies are available, requiring teacher judgment, but all send the same message: "A shrug of the shoulders or an off-the-wall response will not excuse any student from involvement in this lesson."

Q-Card

Prompting Student Answers: Helping Students Who Respond Incorrectly

Cue: Use symbols, words, or phrases to help student recall.

Clue: Use overt reminders such as "starts with . . ."

Probe: Look for reasoning behind an incorrect response or ask for clarity when the response is incomplete.

Rephrase: Pose the same question in different words.

Redirect: Pose the same question to a different student.

Hold accountable later: Later in the lesson, check back with the student who responded incorrectly, to make sure he or she has the correct answer.

Probing. After a student has given a response, teachers can use probes to prompt thinking into the fifth step of the process—revising the answer. Probes can be used following incorrect or incomplete responses as well as following correct responses for which the teacher would like an explanation or rationale. If probes are used with genuine interest in the student's answer, and with respect for the student thinking, they are effective in continuing and expanding the thinking. Students need to be reassured that teachers are probing in order to completely understand student answers and to help move student thinking to higher levels; otherwise the process might feel more like an interrogation and be intimidating to students.

In the case of an incorrect response, teachers may wish to probe for the reasoning behind the response—particularly if the question is above simple recall or knowledge. Using the probe to understand the student's reasoning assists the teacher in making the correction. Probes for this purpose might be, "Can you tell me your reason for saying _____?" "Can you walk me through the process you used to get that answer?"

When a response is incomplete or vague, the teacher may first wish to probe for clarification. A question or statement designed to clarify may ask for a restatement of the response in different words, a definition of a term, or repetition of the question or response. The primary purpose is to help the student think through his or her answer in a manner that eliminates confusion and builds confidence. Standard requests for clarification include the following:

- "Can you tell me what you mean when you say _____?"
- "Can you give me an example of _____?"
- "How are you using the word _____?"
- "Can you say your answer in different words?"

Sometimes a student response may be basically correct but too broad or general. In this case, the teacher may wish to probe for specificity, using the following kinds of questions:

- "Can you be more specific?"
- "Can you give me an example of what you're suggesting?"
- "What facts or evidence can you offer to support your claim?"

Other responses may be correct but incomplete. When a response is only partially correct, the teacher can probe for greater specificity or completeness. Maybe the student has responded with an answer at a lower level than the question demands—which happens as much as 30 to 50 percent of the time. For these responses, probing questions can help students build upon what they do know to reach the higher level of cognition. When probing for completeness, teachers can use the following kinds of prompts:

- "Say more about this."
- "What can you add to this?"
- "What else do you know about _____?"
- "You've told me how they are alike; can you tell me now how they are different?"

Finally, some responses—even if correct—may need an explanation or defense. That is, if a student gives a correct answer, but has incorrect reasoning behind it, the teacher can uncover this with appropriate probes, such as the following:

- "Does that always apply?"
- "Why do you think that is true?"
- "What is the idea behind that?"
- "What evidence do you have to support that conclusion?"

Connie Allen, an elementary school principal in Bowling Green, Kentucky, believes that the demands of today's society, as well as high-stakes testing, make it more important than ever for students to be able to defend and explain their

Q-Card
What to do when a student responds . . . . . . correctly— • use Wait Time 2 (pause for at least three to five seconds) • affirm correctness . . . incompletely— • use Wait Time 2 • probe • rephrase, if needed • then cue or clue if appropriate . . . incorrectly— • use Wait Time 2 • indicate incorrectness, then • rephrase • probe, then • cue or clue, if appropriate, then • redirect question if necessary • make sure the class hears the correct answer • hold original student accountable for correct answer later . . . not at all— • use wait time • rephrase, if possible • cue or clue • redirect, if needed • make sure the class hears the correct answer • hold original student accountable for correct answer later

thinking. A few years ago, she learned of another Kentucky school that began using the S-R-E process (as students answer questions, they make a Statement; give a Reason for their statement; then provide Evidence of why their answer is correct). The school had made the process a schoolwide expectation—from kindergarten on up—and it seemed to be paying off in achievement test scores. "It makes sense," Connie reflects. "To give a reason, you must be thinking. That kind of thinking comes from questioning—good questioning." Connie's school had been using the S-R-E process in the fifth and sixth grades, but after hearing of the other school's success at all grade levels, she said, "We plan to introduce it to our kindergarteners."

This approach is reminiscent of one adopted at Central Park East Secondary School, which has a credo called "The Promise." This credo focuses upon developing the minds of *each and every student*. In practice, this means that students are to learn to ask and answer four key questions in each and every course:

1. From whose viewpoint are we seeing or reading or hearing? From what angle or perspective?

2. How do we know what we know? What's the evidence, and how reliable is it?

3. How are things, events, or people connected to each other? What is the cause and what is the effect? How do they "fit" together?

4. So what? Why does it matter? What does it all mean? Who cares? (Perkins, 1992, p. 169)

As Frances Hunkins (1995) suggests, "Probing's main function is *why*. Why do you say this? Why is this your answer? Why did you employ this method? Why do you make this prediction? Why is this theory appropriate?" (pp. 212-213). Probing prompts students to rethink their responses, engage in reflection, and justify their answers. It helps students make the critical connections essential to new understandings. When students know their teachers will not let them off the hook with a rote answer or praise them for "just trying," they are likely to take greater care in formulating their responses—and to gain more self-confidence as learners.

We believe that the potential of classroom questioning can be realized as we begin acting as if questioning is a way of helping students make connections, a way of scaffolding student thinking—not a tool for getting teacher answers on the floor. When teachers and students alike adopt this view, teacher prompting of student responses supports students who are trying to articulate their understanding of the concept or issue embedded in a question. No longer are prompts seen as embarrassments to students who are spotlighted when the teacher stays with them beyond an initial incorrect or incomplete answer. Rather, teacher prompts convey to students this message: "I care about your current level of thinking and understanding. I want to help you make greater meaning of what we are studying. I care about you and your learning." Teacher prompts also put the rhetoric of high expectations into action by communicating: "I expect each student to have an answer to each question I pose. I hold each student accountable for answering each question. But I will provide support and assistance to students who are struggling to understand." These affective messages can serve as strong motivators for student learning, even as the prompts themselves provide scaffolding for student cognitive processing.

Questions for Reflection

Prompting Student Responses:
Do I assist students in answering each question?

This tool for self-reflection includes reminders of questioning
behaviors that assist students in answering questions.

Questioning Behaviors	Questions for Reflection
Pause after asking the question.	How much time do I give students to think about a question before I call on someone to answer? • Do I allow students three to five seconds? • Are my students aware of Wait Time 1 and why it is important? • Do I provide low and high achievers the same amount of Wait Time 1?
Ask nonrespondents.	Do I give verbal prompts when students have difficulty answering? • Do I restate or replace questions when necessary? • Do I provide cues or clues? • Do students expand their initial responses as a result of my probes? • Do I hold each student accountable for attempting a correct response? • At what point do I redirect questions when students are unable to answer correctly or completely—immediately, or following my prompting?
Pause following the student response.	How long do I pause after a student responds before I speak again? • Do I allow students three to five seconds to complete their answers? • Do I allow the same amount of Wait Time 2 to low and high achievers? • Are students aware of Wait Time 2 and of how and why it is used?
Reflect on related beliefs.	To what extent do you and your students share the following beliefs? • All students can respond to all questions. • All students' answers deserve respect. • Think time is important. • All students can think and reason—beyond rote memory. • Not all questions have one right answer.

References

Barnette, J., Orletsky, S., Sattes, B., & Walsh, J. (1995, April). *Wait-time: Effective and trainable.* Paper presented at the annual meeting of the American Educational Research Association, San Francisco, CA. (ERIC Document Reproduction Service No. ED383706)

Cotton, K. (1988). *Classroom questioning* (School Improvement Series: Research You Can Use, Close-Up #5). Portland, OR: Northwest Regional Educational Laboratory. http://www.nwrel.org/sepd/sirs/3/cu5.html

Hunkins, F. P. (1995). *Teaching thinking through effective questioning* (2nd ed.). Boston: Christopher-Gordon Publishers.

Perkins, D. (1992). *Smart schools: From training memories to educating minds.* Boston: Free Press.

Rowe, M. B. (1986, January-February). Wait time: Slowing down may be a way of speeding up! *Journal of Teacher Education, 37*(1), *43-50.*

Stahl, R. J. (1994). *Using "think-time" and "wait-time" skillfully in the classroom* (ERIC Digest). Bloomington, IN: ERIC Clearinghouse for Social Studies and Social Science Education. (ERIC Document Reproduction Service No. ED370885)

Swift, J. N., Gooding, C. T., & Swift, P. R. (1988). Questions and wait time. In J. T. Dillon (Ed.), *Questioning and discussion: A multidisciplinary study.* Norwood, NJ: Ablex Publishing.

Tobin, K. (1987). The role of wait time in higher cognitive level learning. *Review of Educational Research, 57,* 69-95.

Walsh, J., & Sattes, B. (2003). *QUILT Teacher Manual* (2nd ed.). Charleston, WV: AEL.

Chapter 5:
What Is the Purpose of Teacher Feedback? Bringing Closure *or* Extending Student Thinking and Talking

Focus Questions

How do the various types of teacher feedback direct thinking and learning?

What kinds of questioning strategies serve as scaffolding to help students think more critically and reach deeper understanding?

How can teachers promote quality student-to-student interactions?

> *Schools have been designed to meet the needs of a certain class of learners—those for whom passivity is an acceptable way of learning. Quiet classrooms with docile students, dominated by the teacher's voice, are still perceived as "good" classrooms. That method works for a little over a third of our population.*
>
> —Virginia O'Keefe (1995)

"Quiet classrooms with docile students, dominated by the teacher's voice"—this is the usual goal and outcome of the Initiation-Response-Evaluation/Follow-up model of classroom discourse we explored in Chapter 3. We now turn our attention to the Evaluation/Follow-up component of that model. How teachers react to student responses determines how students process (or don't process) the content on which our questions are focused—and whether or not the "other two thirds" of students are engaged.

Figure 5.1 shows different types of evaluation and follow-up comments that teachers might provide after a student responds to a question. Included are the likely impacts of each type of feedback and contexts in which each type might be appropriate. In each case, the purpose for teacher talk depends on the desired impact on student thinking and learning. During recitation, teachers might use praise and feedback (positive, negative, and corrective) to reinforce student understanding and long-term retention of knowledge. During discussion, teachers might use radically different kinds of responses to motivate and support students as they grapple with issues, interact with one another, and raise their own questions. The primary intent of teacher talk during discussion is to

Figure 5.1

Relationship Between Teacher Reaction and Student Thinking and Learning

Teacher Reaction to Student Response	Impact on Student Thinking and Learning	Appropriate Context
Prompts and probes as needed, then gives clear and definitive praise or positive or corrective feedback.	Students are left with a complete and correct understanding.	Recitation
Provides positive or corrective feedback and asks questions or makes comments that help students connect new knowledge to prior knowledge.	Students make connections that will enable them to store and retain new knowledge for future use.	Recitation
Asks follow-up question to "correct" student answer.	Student extends or expands thoughts, going deeper or making new connections.	Recitation or Discussion
Redirects question to another student.	Student elaborates on what initial responder said (during recitation) or offers alternative point of view (during discussion).	Recitation or Discussion
Makes a personal observation, asks a question out of perplexity, redirects to another student, or uses some other "alternative" move (no praise or positive, negative, or corrective feedback).	Students raise their own questions and/or offer different perspectives; their conversations move into "new territory."	Discussion
Summarizes student comments to bring tentative closure to discussion; poses questions that continue to perplex or remained unanswered.	Students continue to think about the question and its implications beyond a given class period.	Discussion
Offers simple, monosyllabic, monotonic feedback.	Students passively accept (or ignore) "correct" answers.	Almost Never
Fails to provide clear feedback to a convergent question.	Students are confused as to whether a given student answer is correct or not.	Never

facilitate and sustain student conversation rather than to evaluate student answers. In either context, teacher reactions to student responses deserve thoughtful attention.

Teacher Feedback Provides Direction for Student Learning

Let's begin with a deeper look at the use of feedback in recitations, where the questions are convergent (have a limited number of correct answers) and the purpose is to help students retain knowledge and deepen understandings of that knowledge. As teachers, we have three primary jobs in a well-orchestrated recitation: (1) to assure that all students know whether or not a given answer is right or wrong; (2) to ensure that all students are aware of the most complete, appropriate, and correct response to each question; and (3) to help students connect new knowledge to prior learnings and experiences and help move it into long-term memory.

All student answers to questions in recitation require and deserve the appropriate type of teacher feedback (Figure 5.2 presents the standard alternatives). To withhold feedback from students is to devalue their answers. Research findings suggest that low achievers are *less* likely to find out from teachers how they're doing than are high achievers. Yet research also tells us low-achieving students require *more* feedback, both positive and corrective, than do other students. Why? Because they often lack the positive academic self-concept that would enable them to better tolerate ambiguity.

Verbal feedback from a teacher is a type of formative assessment, an opportunity to let students know the areas in which they are doing well and to help them improve in areas of need. As with any type of assessment, verbal feedback is more effective when teacher and students share an understanding of the criteria on which performance will be evaluated. Typically, teacher and students alike look to the content of a student's response ("Was the answer right?") to determine its quality. We suggest that classroom questioning is more complex than this type of assessment suggests.

Questions solicit both knowledge and *processing* of knowledge at a designated cognitive level. Further, the effective question-answer exchange does not always involve a single teacher question and a single student response. Rather, when a correct answer is not given, effective teachers prompt students to provide answers that are either more correct, more complete, or at the desired cognitive level. Oral questioning episodes also provide students with the rare opportunity to practice skills in public speaking. All of this occurs in a classroom context in which other students are to listen actively and learn from the teacher-student exchange.

In recognition of these complexities, our rubric for assessing student answers (see Figure 5.3) includes four components (knowledge, thinking, verbal skills, and responses to follow-up questions) and provides criteria for assessing each. Teachers can use such a rubric with students to give them a picture of what an exemplary response looks and sounds like. Teachers can also use the rubric as a guide in providing specific, clear, and contingent feedback. The more specific our feedback, the more beneficial it will be to our students' learning. The rubric shown here is generic; it is not specific to any subject area or grade level. We encourage teachers to use it as a model for developing a rubric for their own classrooms and students.

Figure 5.2

Types and Uses of Teacher Feedback in Recitation

Type of Feedback	Characteristics	When To Use
Positive	Confirms the correctness of the student's answer.	When the student offers a complete and correct response to a fairly simple, convergent question.
Corrective	Communicates the answer is either incorrect or incomplete and guides the student toward a correct understanding and response; may redirect question to another student or, in some cases, provide the answer for students. For a complex question, teacher returns to first student to assure that the student now understands.	When the student's answer continues to be incorrect or incomplete after teacher prompts.
Negative	Informs the student that the answer is not acceptable.	When engaged in drill and practice of simple facts, teacher may give a simple "thumbs down" to a wrong answer or state "No, that's incorrect."
Praise	Affirms the correctness of the student's answer in a laudatory fashion.	Reserve for "exceptional" answers, usually to questions that are above the remembering level.
Criticism	Rejects the student's answer in a negative and critical manner.	Almost never
Absent	Provides no comment following a student's answer.	Almost never

Figure 5.3

QUILT Rubric for Assessing Student Answers

Score	Knowledge	Thinking	Verbal Skills	Responses to Follow-Up Questions
3	Shows an excellent understanding of what the question is about. Includes correct and complete facts, data, concepts. Uses appropriate vocabulary and terminology. Asks clarifying questions, if necessary.	Demonstrates the level of thinking called for by the question. Shows a complete understanding of the ideas and concepts (provides evidence, examples, patterns, or relationships). Relates answer to previous student and teacher comments as appropriate.	Speaks clearly and projects voice well. Speaks to entire class, not to teacher only. Uses complete and grammatically correct sentences. Organizes and sequences words so that meaning is clear.	Formulates a correct answer to cues, clues, or prompts. Extends or elaborates on initial answer when invited to do so. Corrects initial answer (if incorrect) when afforded time, feedback, or prompts.
2	Shows a basic understanding of what the question is about. Includes some correct facts, data, concepts. Uses acceptable vocabulary but is sometimes careless in choice of words. Is hesitant to ask clarifying questions if needed.	Approximates the level of thinking called for by the question. Shows some understanding of the ideas and concepts (provides minimal evidence or examples). Refers to previous student and teacher comments, if cued.	Speaks fairly clearly and projects voice adequately. Speaks mainly to teacher. Uses mostly complete and correct sentences. Organizes and sequences words so that meaning is fairly clear.	Formulates a reasonable answer to cues, clues, or prompts. Adds very little to original answer when pressed to do so. Partially corrects initial answer (if incorrect) when afforded time, feedback, or prompts.
1	Shows little or no understanding of what the question is about. Provides incorrect facts, data, concepts. Uses low-level vocabulary. Fails to ask clarifying questions, if needed.	Does not respond with the appropriate level of thinking. Shows little or no understanding of the ideas and concepts. Does not recall previous student and teacher comments, even when cued.	Mumbles; cannot be heard. Fails to make eye contact with anyone. Offers one-word responses. Fails to convey meaning.	Fails to provide correct responses to cues. Is unable to add to original answer. Seems unable to understand why initial answer is incomplete or incorrect.

Effective Praise

Praise is a special type of feedback that extends beyond mere assessment of a student's answer. It is often viewed as a positive reinforcement for both learning and behavior. Praise includes positive teacher affect, embodies a value statement, and gives students information concerning their status. Teachers use praise, consciously and unconsciously, to motivate their students.

> The focus must be on the quality of praise. When quantity is the major emphasis, praise does not have the effect of reinforcement, thereby defeating the teacher's intent.
>
> —Richard Kindsvatter, William Wilen, & Margaret Ishler (1996, p. 208)

The value of praise has long been a focus for researchers. Brophy (1981) reviewed dozens of studies and concluded that praise does not always reinforce student learning or behavior. He identifies three variables associated with the effectiveness of praise: frequency, distribution, and quality.

Frequency. The effectiveness of praise depends, in part, on the frequency and consistency with which it is used. The desired frequency varies with the age and developmental and ability levels of students. Younger students require praise more often than older students; in fact, as students progress through school, they require increasingly less of this type of reinforcement. Lower-achieving students, as previously mentioned, need more feedback—therefore, more praise—than other students.

Overall, Brophy found that teachers use praise infrequently, seldom commending students for providing good answers; however, other researchers have found that overuse of praise dilutes its effectiveness. Brophy's findings suggest that use of praise is dependent on individual teachers' personalities and styles. Often, our praise is not an intentional, planned reinforcement, but a spontaneous reaction to student behavior.

Distribution. Brophy found that the students who most need praise, low-achieving students, do not receive their "fair share." High achievers receive more teacher praise than other students—and not necessarily because they are correct more often. Even when low achievers answer correctly, they are less likely to be praised than are high achievers. Other research suggests that teacher praise varies with the amount of effort the student appears to be making. Because teachers frequently perceive low achievers to make little effort, these students are at a disadvantage when compared to high achievers (Brophy, 1981).

Quality. Praise must meet certain criteria to function effectively as a reinforcer of student learning. Brophy offers four criteria: (1) contingent on performance of a stipulated behavior, (2) specific, (3) credible, and (4) sincere.

1. *Contingency*. Praise must be contingent on performance of a known, desired behavior for it to function as a reinforcer. Most often we do not use praise this way. According to Brophy, teachers often shift the criteria. What is praised one day may not be praised another. Occasionally, teachers praise students even when their answers are incorrect. This occurs most frequently with low-achieving students, who usually "see through" this false (though well-intentioned) praise and find it demeaning or discouraging.

2. *Specificity*. For praise to function as a reinforcer, it must be specific. Brophy notes that teachers are specific only about five percent of the time.

3. *Credibility*. To be effective, the praise must be valid and based on evidence. Further, students must believe the praise to be true.

4. *Sincerity*. Praise must sound sincere for students to accept it as a reinforcer. Brophy writes that teachers sometimes contradict their verbal praise with their nonverbal expressions. This occurs more frequently with students deemed by teachers to be "behavior problems."

In view of the widespread misunderstanding and misuse of praise, it is not surprising that praise does not correlate positively with student achievement gains except in the case of low-SES/low-ability students in the early grades. Brophy, however, argues that if praise were used effectively, it would serve as a reinforcer and would impact student achievement in a positive manner.

The rubric presented in Figure 5.3 can help teachers overcome common pitfalls and use praise more effectively. The rubric provides standards that address Brophy's four criteria for effective praise (contingency, specificity, credibility, and sincerity). Stipulated are the expected characteristics of student responses—knowledge that is correct and complete, thinking that demonstrates a designated level of processing, use of good verbal skills, and attention to follow-up questions. Explicit use of the rubric therefore enables *contingency* in praise statements. Also, because the rubric stipulates the qualities constituting a high level of performance in four different areas, it enables teachers to be *specific* with their praise. When students know the standards for assessment, praise becomes more *credible* because it is linked to shared expectations. And finally, linking praise statements to known standards can make teacher praise authentic and more *sincere*. When praise is contingent, specific, credible, and sincere, students are more likely to listen to, value, and respond to teacher feedback.

The rubric and Brophy's four criteria can be used in tandem to ensure that all types of teacher feedback, including praise, are perceived as "real" and meaningful. We suggest that teachers not only develop and use such a rubric as a tool for themselves, but that they share the rubric with students and parents. This can improve communications among these vital partners in students' learning and support students in becoming more metacognitive (a skill that will be explored in Chapter 6).

Effective Feedback of Other Types

Effective feedback can keep the class focused on questions and responses, rather than on the personalities of the students offering the answers, and can thereby spotlight the academic purposes of class interactions. Properly used, feedback becomes a teaching tool not only for the responding student but also for the entire class. All students profit from feedback that is instructive, instructional, and focused. Further, they learn to listen when teacher feedback is of this nature.

While feedback is usually verbal, it need not be so. A teacher may also use signals, particularly during a recitation. A nod of the head obviously signals "correct." This may be followed by a question designed to amplify the student response.

Remember, we are focusing upon the use of feedback in the context of recitation, where convergent questions are seeking answers that can be evaluated as to their correctness. When we formulate feedback by reference to a rubric and a set of criteria, we are more likely to effectively discharge two of the instructional responsibilities we mentioned earlier: (1) letting the individual respondent know whether a proffered answer is right or wrong, and (2) leaving all students in the class with an understanding of the most complete, correct, and appropriate answer(s) for each question. But what of the third "job" we suggested—helping students make connections that will enable long-term retention of knowledge?

In Chapter 4, we examined techniques that can be used to help students make connections that lead to a correct response—prompts, cues, clues, and probes. It is good instruction to help students continue the process of connection-making even after a correct answer is "on the floor." This is a powerful technique for reinforcing new learnings.

For example, imagine that a biology teacher poses this question to a class: "What are the differences between plant and animal cells?" After three to four seconds of Wait Time 1, the teacher calls on a student, who answers: "Umm . . . A plant cell has a cell wall . . . and it also contains chloroplasts. Animal cells don't have either of those." The teacher waits four seconds (Wait Time 2), and the student adds: "A plant cell has a regular shape to it, but an animal cell does not." After another three seconds, the student says: "And plant cells have large vacuoles. Animal cells don't." The teacher waits again to be certain that the student has completed her thoughts. She then smiles, nods at the student and responds: "Yes. You correctly named the four major differences between the two types of cells. I really appreciate your speaking loudly enough that we could all hear you." The teacher might then ask her students to draw their own simple sketch of these two types of cells; after a couple of minutes, she could then call for two volunteers to share their sketches on the whiteboard.

At this point, the teacher might transition by posing a divergent question: "Why do you think plant and animal cells developed so differently? Take a few seconds to come up with at least one reason why you think this happens." The teacher provides 12 to 15 seconds for student thinking. She then steps to the board and says: "Let's make a list of your theories. Remember, at this point, there are no right or wrong answers. I'm just interested in your thinking about why these two types of cells have developed so differently." As students formulate their own answers and listen to their peers, the process of connection making is taken to another level—and the probability of long-term retention is enhanced. The students are using the knowledge in an arena in which they are able to connect a known (the differences between plant and animal cells) to other things they have learned or sensed. They engage in active speculation.

Remember David Perkins' three goals of education?

- Retention of knowledge
- Understanding of knowledge
- Active use of knowledge

In this biology class, the students' understanding of an important distinction grows as they use this knowledge to theorize and speculate. This is a practical example of how the asking and answering of higher-level questions can enhance retention and recall. Students are much more likely to remember key concepts after such a meaningful discussion than they would be in a class where the teacher continued in recitation style to her next, and perhaps unrelated, question.

Beyond Feedback: Inviting Students to Elaborate or Piggyback

As teachers, we can validate student answers as correct or provide corrective feedback to assist students in correcting wrong answers. In the strictest sense of the term, we will have used feedback correctly. However, by taking this narrow approach, we forgo opportunities to help our students extend and expand their thinking. Elaboration is the process whereby an individual continues his or her thinking by going deeper, making new connections, or raising additional questions.

What can we do to facilitate student elaboration? As discussed in Chapter 4, we can consistently use Wait Time 2—affording students the time and the "space" within classroom recitations and discussion to say more about what's on their minds. Additionally, we can pose follow-up questions. Here is a list of generic questions that invite student elaboration:

- How did you decide that?
- How did you arrive at that?
- Elaborate for others in the class so they can check their thinking.

- What made you think of that?
- Tell us about the procedure you used.
- Can you justify that?
- What steps did you use to arrive at this solution?
- Tell us in "eighth-grade" language (or whatever grade level you are teaching).
- What evidence can you offer to support this point of view?
- Can you think of another way of attacking this problem?

This listing is only suggestive of the questions that may cause students to think more about a topic.

Q-Card

Alternatives to Feedback During a Discussion

1. Make a simple declarative statement.

   Example: "Not everything you read is true."

2. Paraphrase what you heard the student say.

   Example: "So you think that . . . (paraphrase the student's statement)."

3. Describe your state of mind.

   Example: "I'm confused about what you're saying."

4. Invite the student to elaborate.

   Example: "Maybe you could give some examples to help us better understand."

5. Invite the student to ask a question.

   Example: "Do you need to ask a question to clarify your thinking?"

6. Invite the class to ask the student a question.

   Example: "Does anyone have a question about Carla's statement?"

7. Be deliberately silent.

   (Use Wait Time 2.)

Alternatives to Teacher Feedback in Discussion

Feedback of all types serves to close or terminate a student's answering. This is an important function of feedback during a recitation, when pacing is important. In this context, feedback informs the student as to the merit of a response. However, during a discussion, where there is no single "right" answer, simple feedback can interfere with—and even shut down—student thinking. In this context, all types of feedback should be used sparingly and carefully. One purpose of true discussion is to offer students the climate and opportunities to develop confidence in their expressions. Discussion should wean students from dependence on a teacher's affirmation or correction and move them toward independent thinking and expression.

James T. Dillon (1988) offers seven widely accepted alternatives to feedback in a discussion (see Q-Card). Most teachers find it difficult to refrain from feedback during discussion because all of us have been conditioned that "immediate feedback is important"—and human nature is to give positive reinforcement to those who agree with our thinking. But we must learn to use alternatives to feedback if we wish to sustain student thinking over the course of an extended discussion. One of our workshop participants suggested that we "get out the duct tape" if necessary!

Elaboration and Redirection

After providing appropriate feedback (or no feedback, in the case of true discussion), the teacher can move the class into what can become the most interesting part of a questioning episode: the segment during which both the responding student and observing students are invited to extend, expand, or elaborate upon the initial answer or, in the case of responses to divergent questions, to offer alternative responses. Teachers can use the techniques of elaboration and redirection to accomplish these ends.

Through elaboration, teachers encourage students to expand upon what may have been a correct but very abbreviated response. The purpose of elaboration is to engage the student and his or her classmates in a conversation, using the initial response as a springboard for thinking. This may result in broadening the response at the initial level of cognition, or it may lead students to higher levels of thinking. In either case, teacher and students learn to *piggyback* on initial responses as they enter into meaningful dialogues.

To increase the number of student participants in the dialogue, the teacher can *redirect* the initial question to another student. Redirection involves posing the question in its initial form to someone other than the initial respondent. Obviously, all questions cannot, or should not, be redirected. Convergent questions that have been correctly and completely answered are not candidates for redirection. Divergent questions, for which there are multiple correct responses or alternatives, invite redirection.

If I could select just one area of the questioning process for improvement, I would probably point toward the area of pro-cessing student responses simply because it's in this stage that relationships are built. And confidence is built there. Providing the appropriate feedback to children helps them (if you do it in the right way) to feel more confident and to expand their learning. To me, it has the potential to be a stimulus for more learning—for them to be open to more learning. Preparing and presenting and prompting—these are all important. But in the processing, what a teacher does with what a student gives makes tons of difference in a student's wanting to continue to learn.

—Margaret Allen, Director of Professional Development, Montgomery, Alabama

Teachers Can Encourage and Support Student-to-Student Interactions

The real goal of discussion is to encourage student-to-student interactions; however, most students have had little training or experience in "true discussion." Classroom observers report that most students lack this expertise because they have not been encouraged to develop it (Dillon, 1988; Brookfield & Preskill, 1999). Teacher encouragement can take the form of intentional modeling, where the teacher herself becomes a discussant and engages with students in a conversational, as opposed to a pedagogical, mode.

What discrete supports can we provide to engage students in discussion? Many who have studied classroom interactions, including Stephen Brookfield and Stephen Preskill, advocate overt teaching of conversational skills. One strategy they offer is to introduce students to a variety of "conversational moves." A teacher might record these "moves" on index cards (one on each card) and randomly distribute the cards to students, instructing them to practice the one listed on their card during a discussion session. Alternate strategies suggested by Brookfield and Preskill (1999, pp. 101-102) include the following:

- Ask a question or make a comment that shows you are interested in what another person has said.

- Ask a question or make a comment that encourages someone else to elaborate on something that person has said.

- Make a comment that underscores a link between two people's contributions. Make this link explicit in your comment.

- Use body language (in a slightly exaggerated way) to show interest in what different speakers are saying.

- Make a comment indicating that you found another person's ideas interesting or useful. Be specific as to why this was the case.

- Contribute something that builds on or springs from what someone else has said. Be explicit about the way you are building on someone else's thoughts.

- Make a comment that at least partly paraphrases a point someone has already made.

- At an appropriate moment, ask the group for a minute's silence to slow the pace of conversation and give you and others time to think.

- Find a way to express appreciation for the enlightenment you have gained from the discussion. Try to be specific about what it was that helped you understand something better.

- Disagree with someone in a respectful and constructive way.

As students think about their assigned roles during a given discussion, they not only contribute actively to the discourse, but they also develop new metacognitive skills.

Use of "conversational move" cards is an activity that should be repeated over time so that students can develop competence and confidence in using different moves at appropriate times. Further, we suggest that you help your students reflect on their involvement as each discussion comes to an end. You might ask students to respond, first in writing, to the following questions:

- What did you contribute to this class discussion?
- How, specifically, did your statements affect what your classmates said following your contribution?
- What did you learn about the process of discussion from today's class dialogue?
- Think about the class as a whole. What can we do to improve the quality of our discussions?

Following individual reflection, you can initiate a whole-group discussion by asking students what they think went well and writing their responses on the board. Then, ask them to share their thinking about how to improve discussions in this class.

How else can a teacher encourage student interactions with one another? In his engaging book, *Developing More Curious Minds,* John Barell (2003) offers a number of practical suggestions:

- Arrange the classroom so that students can see one another's faces.
- Encourage students to talk to one another instead of to the teacher. (In order to accomplish this, the teacher can prohibit hand-raising and can sit down with the students rather than standing or sitting at the teacher desk.)
- Search for other points of view that may contradict prevailing attitudes. For example, try a role reversal: "Will you and Rod switch sides and argue each other's point of view?" (pp. 102-103)

> How teachers guide students to interact with one another during instruction will influence the way students learn, the attitudes they form about the subject matter and the instructor, and the perceptions they have about themselves and others.
>
> —Roger T. Johnson and David W. Johnson (1985, p. 22)

These are but a sampling of techniques that teachers can employ to open up their classrooms for increased student-to-student interaction.

Active Listening and Openness to Students Enable Effective Feedback and Elaboration

Guiding students in discussion—and using performance criteria to guide our own verbal feedback—is not easy. These challenging tasks require us to listen actively and attentively to student answers—and to be open to hearing what each student is saying. This means we must stop listening solely to hear *our answer* and listen instead, as James T. Dillon advocates, with interest in the *student's answer*. Active listening and openness are prerequisite to the formation of contingent, credible, sincere feedback during recitation—and to appropriate reactions to student comments during discussion.

Attentive listening is never an easy task—it consumes psychic energy at a rate that tires and surprises me. But it is made easier when I am holding back my own authoritative impulses. When I suspend, for just a while, my inner chatter about what I am going to say next, I open room within myself to receive the external conversation.

—Parker Palmer (1998, p. 135)

Effective teacher listening behaviors are critical if quality questions are to result in productive teacher-student interactions. Richard Kindsvatter and colleagues (1996) identify seven components of listening that teachers can use to communicate interest and to signify that student comments are important:

1. *Eye contact*—looking directly at the speaker and maintaining eye contact

2. *Facial expressions*—using a variety of appropriate facial expressions, such as smiling or demonstrating surprise or excitement

3. *Body posture*—using gestures such as hand signals; maintaining body posture that signifies openness to students' ideas

4. *Physical distance*—adjusting one's position in the classroom according to one's condition of instruction; for example, moving closer to a student who is speaking (or to a student who is less engaged)

5. *Silence*—being quiet while a student is speaking—not interrupting; honoring Wait Time 2 after a student stops speaking

6. *Verbal acknowledgements*—using brief, appropriate verbal acknowledgements such as "go ahead," "yes," or "I understand"

7. *Subsummaries*—restating or paraphrasing the main ideas presented by students during lengthy discussions (p. 215)

One of the most powerful ways to reinforce student contributions is to refer back to them later. This strategy—particularly effective during discussion, when positive feedback and praise are inappropriate—depends upon our attentive listening and our focus on individual students.

Courtesy and Respect Create an Environment for Student Acceptance of Feedback

It's all about respect. If our students are to accept our feedback and use it to advance their learning, they must believe that we respect them as learners and as human beings—and they must respect us. It's that simple—or, some would say, it's that difficult.

What are the cardinal principles for developing a classroom environment that is defined by respectful relationships between and among teacher and students? Do you remember the six norms introduced in Chapter 1? Two of these norms address the issue of respect.

- We learn from one another when we listen with attention and respect.
- When we share talk time, we demonstrate respect, and we learn from one another.

We submit that the best way for teachers to promote respectfulness across the classroom is for us to model these two norms—that is, first, to listen to students with attention and respect, and second, to share our talk time with them and let them know that we are interested in them and in learning from them. These are two cardinal principles for creating a classroom environment grounded in respect: *active and respectful listening* and *active demonstration of interest in each and every child.* In order for these principles to produce the desired outcome, we must adhere to them sincerely and consistently over time.

Another key for creating an environment that supports learning through feedback is *thoughtfulness.* Barell (1995) writes about two aspects of thoughtfulness:

> This word [thoughtfulness] combines two aspects of our lives: intellectual or cognitive operations plus feelings, attitudes, and dispositions. Thoughtfulness, therefore, calls upon us as educators to help students recognize the attitudes they have toward themselves as thinkers ("Do I have confidence I can solve most problems?") and their attitudes toward others ("Am I open to other people's ideas?"). Without both cognitive and affective components, we in schools too often focus upon the one aspect of intelligent behavior that is more easily measurable and planned for. (p. 6)

When we teachers model both the cognitive and the affective dimensions of thoughtfulness, we demonstrate our openness to students' ideas and ways of thinking. In a classroom where both teacher and students embrace the affective dimension of thoughtfulness, students will be much more open to feedback from teachers and from their peers.

The Challenge Is to Engage the Silent Two-Thirds in Learning and Thinking

This chapter opened with Virginia O'Keefe's claim that "quiet classrooms with docile students" work for a "little over a third of our population." The behaviors associated with the Evaluation/Follow-up stage of questioning—skillful use of appropriate feedback in recitation (or alternatives, in discussion) and invitation to student elaboration or piggybacking—can serve as catalysts for engaging "the other two-thirds" of our students. This is particularly true when these teacher behaviors are used in the context of a positive, respectful climate, one in which students feel they are being heard and valued. Facilitating students to respond to teacher questions requires a great deal of teacher skill and commitment; however, providing students with the competence and confidence to raise their own questions is even more challenging. This more proactive type of student engagement is addressed in the next chapter.

Questions for Reflection
Assessing and Using Student Answers:
How do I respond to each student answer?

This tool for self-reflection includes reminders
of effective responses and feedback to student questions.

Questioning Behaviors	Questions for Reflection
Provide appropriate feedback.	What type of feedback do I give? • Do I give positive feedback for correct answers? • Do I use praise appropriately? • Do I give students a chance to correct their own wrong answers? • Do I leave all students with a correct understanding? • Do I provide high and low achievers with equal amounts of feedback?
Expand and use correct responses.	Do students expand upon correct answers? • Do I use or expand upon student answers? Do I refer to student answers later in a lesson? • Do I redirect questions to encourage students to think of alternative correct responses?
Elicit students' reactions and questions.	Do students interact with one another and initiate questions? • What techniques are used to promote student interactions? • Do students initiate substantive questions during class?
Reflect on related beliefs.	To what extent do you and your students share the following beliefs? • Students will ask questions when confused or curious. • Divergent thinking is important. • Not all questions have one right answer.

References

Barell, J. (1995). *Teaching for thoughtfulness: Classroom strategies to enrich intellectual development* (2nd ed.). White Plains, NY: Longman Publishers.

Barell, J. (2003). *Developing more curious minds.* Alexandria, VA: Association for Supervision and Curriculum Development.

Brophy, J. (1981, Spring). Teacher praise: A functional analysis. *Review of Educational Research, 1*(1), 5-32.

Brookfield, S. D., & Preskill, S. (1999). *Discussion as a way of teaching: Tools and techniques for democratic classrooms.* San Francisco: Jossey-Bass.

Dillon, J. T. (1988). *Questioning and teaching: A manual of practice.* New York: Teachers College Press.

Hunkins, F. P. (1995). *Teaching thinking through effective questioning* (2nd ed.). Boston: Christopher-Gordon Publishers.

Johnson, R. T., & Johnson, D. W. (1985). Student-student interaction: Ignored but powerful. *Journal of Teacher Education, 36,* 22-26.

Kindsvatter, R., Wilen, W., & Ishler, M. (1996). *Dynamics of effective teaching* (3rd ed.). White Plains, NY: Longman.

Oakes, J., & Lipton, M. (1999). *Teaching to change the world.* New York: McGraw-Hill College.

O'Keefe, V. (1995). *Speaking to think, thinking to speak: The importance of talk in the learning process.* Portsmouth, NH: Boynton/Cook Publishers.

Palmer, P. (1998). *The courage to teach: Exploring the inner landscape of a teacher's life.* San Francisco: Jossey-Bass.

Perkins, D. (1992). *Smart schools: Better thinking and learning for every child.* New York: The Free Press.

Chapter 6:
How Do Students Become More Effective Thinkers and Learners? Teaching Students to Generate Questions

Focus Questions

What are the connections between students' questioning, thinking, learning, and achievement?

What do we need to teach students about the art of formulating questions and using effective questioning strategies?

How can we create a classroom culture that encourages and supports student questioning?

A bright-eyed, 10th-grade student in a large suburban high school reflects on what helps her learn: "When I am able to come up with questions of my own, it's easier for me to understand and remember what we're studying." This student has incredible insight into the relationship between questioning, thinking, and learning. When a student grapples to create her own questions about content, she is engaging in the process of meaning making—a standard definition of thinking. By formulating questions, learners connect new information to old and thereby experience learning as understanding (Oakes & Lipton, 1999). Cognitive researchers are finding that students who make connections between new content and personal experience are engaging in productive and long-term learning. Additionally, these students develop intrinsic motivation and the skills of lifelong learning (Wells, 2001; Perkins, 1992).

However, the goal of helping *every* student become an effective questioner is somewhat daunting. Only a few seem to be born questioners, possessing the skills, curiosity, and self-confidence that prompt them to wonder, formulate questions, and proactively vie to get their question on the floor. Other students enter school with real handicaps in this area, often because they live in homes where adults do not model communication skills or encourage children to practice their own. In our experience, most students possess adequate communication skills but minimal motivation to interact around academic topics. The range of prior student knowledge, skills, and attitudes makes the development of *questioning students* a complex challenge. The challenge is exacerbated by accountability measures that press teachers to focus on content—not process. How, then, can teachers simultaneously develop *questioning students* and improve student achievement?

In *Developing More Curious Minds,* John Barell (2003) writes about the nature of good questions:

- A good question reflects a genuine desire to find out, a deep feeling for wanting to know more than we already know.

- A good question helps us think; [it is] one that is transcendent, one that helps us move beyond the immediate data or experience. (pp. 59-62)

Barell challenges teachers to create a culture of inquisitiveness, and to help students develop the skills requisite to asking good questions. He suggests modeling as a powerful strategy for attaining these twin goals. We can model inquisitiveness as well as good question-asking for our students.

A helpful first step is to "break down" the challenge into its discrete components. A growing research base is establishing a relationship between academic achievement and student questioning in at least four interrelated areas:

1. metacognitive knowledge
2. knowledge and use of question formulation skills
3. curiosity, inquisitiveness, and sense of wonder
4. confidence and self-efficacy

The first two of these fall within the cognitive domain; that is, they deal with what students know and are able to do. The latter ones are about feelings and attitudes—supportive habits of mind that develop in the affective dimension.

In this chapter, as we look at each of these dimensions, we examine research on the nature and scope of associated student behaviors; suggest classroom conditions (norms, structures, and climate) that encourage questioning behaviors; and present selected strategies and formats for helping students develop the knowledge, skills, and dispositions that foster higher levels of questioning, thinking, learning, and achievement.

Questioning Is Key to Metacognition

John Flavell, a Stanford University psychologist, coined the term *metacognition* in the late 1970s to name the process of thinking about one's own thinking and learning. Since then, cognitive scientists have focused considerable time and attention on studying this phenomenon, which emphasizes making students more aware of and responsible for their own knowledge and thought.

The National Research Council identifies metacognition as one of three key factors in student learning for which there is a solid research base (Bransford, Brown, & Cocking, 2000, pp. 14-19). David Perkins (1995) author of *Outsmarting IQ,* makes a strong case that through teaching students metacognitive strategies, we can impact their IQ scores.

Left to ourselves we will not usually become skilled thinkers. Just left alone and told to think, our students will not gain the skill. We may be wired for thinking activity, but we require instruction in how to employ our circuitry in particular ways to make meaning. David Perkins has argued this point, indicating that while "everyday thinking, like ordinary walking, is a natural performance mastered by all, good thinking, like running the 100-yard dash, is a technical performance, full of artifice." Therefore, good thinking and effective questioning require deliberate conscious effort, require practice, modification of action, and reflection on action.

—Francis P. Hunkins (1996, p. 17)

Authors of the revised Bloom Taxonomy included metacognition— "knowledge about cognition in general as well as awareness of and knowledge about one's own cognition"—as one of four dimensions of knowledge (Anderson & Krathwohl, 2001, p. 55). They cite recent research findings that relate "students' knowledge about their own cognition and control of their own cognition" to learning and achievement (p. 43). The revised taxonomy presents three components of metacognitive knowledge:

1. Strategic knowledge—knowledge of general strategies for knowledge, thinking, and problem solving

2. Knowledge about cognitive tasks—knowledge of various cognitive tasks and knowledge of when and why to use strategies

3. Self-knowledge—knowledge about self in relation to both cognitive and motivational components of performance (Anderson & Krathwohl, 2001, p. 56)

At the heart of each of these is the learner's ability to formulate questions. Teachers can help students develop all three components of metacognitive knowledge by using formats that call upon students' abilities to ask and answer questions. Two such formats are reciprocal teaching and pair problem solving.

Reciprocal Teaching

Reciprocal teaching, a strategy for increasing reading comprehension, teaches students the skills of generating questions, clarifying, summarizing, and predicting—and how to use these in the context of a collaborative, text-based conversation. Developed by Palincsar and Brown (1984), the strategy engages teachers and students in interactive dialogue for the purpose of developing meaning from a text.

The classroom teacher selects a passage from the text, basing the length of the reading on the students' ability levels. The text selection can be as short as one sentence for some students. The structure for reciprocal teaching consists of three steps, which must be followed carefully if the process is to work (Swicegood & Parsons, 1989, p. 6).

1. Students summarize what they have read and generate questions about the passage. The teacher names one student to role-play "teacher" and to question classmates. During the ensuing discussion, students talk about the details of the reading selection, draw conclusions, and make predictions about what is likely to occur next.

2. The teacher functions as a model and a coach to assist students in learning good questioning. Initially, the teacher provides verbal cues to help students generate good questions (e.g., *Think of something about the main character that might be interesting to talk about*) or suggests questions that students are likely to answer correctly, which develops their confidence in answering.

   As students become more competent and confident in question generation, the teacher transfers primary responsibility to them and coaches students as they continually improve their questioning. During this more mature stage of the process, the teacher actively listens to understand the reasoning of the students and intervenes when scaffolding is required.

3. Students are encouraged to ask questions for clarification (e.g., when they need a definition for a new vocabulary word).

An extensive research base confirms the effectiveness of reciprocal teaching in improving the reading comprehension of children with a wide range of learning needs, but this process is successful only when teachers "buy in" to the belief that collaboration among students and teachers to construct meaning produces higher-quality learning (Palincsar & Brown, 1984).

Pair Problem Solving

This strategy, devised for mathematics and science classrooms, focuses on problem solving. Students are organized into pairs. One student is designated to think aloud, talking through the problem and sharing his or her thoughts with the partner. The second student has two responsibilities: first, to understand the partner's thinking—right or wrong—by asking questions to get behind the thinking, and second, not to intervene, even if the partner makes mistakes. At the end of the problem solving, the students discuss the problem, then switch roles for the next problem.

Jack Lochhead, who with Arthur Whimbey (1982) developed the strategy, believes metacognitive awareness and reflection are important aspects of effective problem solving. He admits that it is difficult for students to engage in these processes and, at the same time, keep their attention focused on the problem itself. In pair problem solving, the listening partner helps the speaker surface his thoughts and make sense of them by posing questions for clarification. "Thoughts that otherwise would stream by in the rapids of moment-to-moment cognition" are captured (Perkins, 1995, 141-142).

Pair problem solving, like reciprocal teaching, engages students in thinking about their thinking. Likewise, it has been extensively researched and found to produce substantial learning gains for all learners, including students with learning disabilities (Whimbey & Lochhead, 1982.) The success of both strategies depends upon a teacher's commitment to the process, teacher modeling, coaching of students in the posing of questions, and, of course, student ability to generate good questions.

Effective Question Generation Skills Improve Student Achievement

Not all students automatically know how to generate good questions; however, all students can be taught how to formulate questions—and research provides insights into how best to go about this instructional task. Much of this research has been conducted in the context of reading comprehension because of the centrality of reading to learning in all academic areas. In 2000, the National Reading Panel looked at 203 studies about "instruction of text comprehension" and identified seven scientifically based research strategies that improve comprehension, three of which specifically relate to questioning:

- *Recognition of story structure,* which requires the reader to ask and answer *who, what, where, when,* and *why* questions about the plot and, in some cases, to map out the timeline, characters, and events in stories.

- *Question answering* in which the reader answers questions posed by the teacher and is given feedback on the correctness.

- *Question generation* in which the reader asks himself or herself *what, when, where, why, what will happen, how,* and *who* questions.

The panel found the strongest scientifically based evidence for the third of these strategies—asking readers to generate questions while reading. The report concludes: "When teachers teach these strategies, their students learn them and improve their reading comprehension" (pp. 4-6).

> Give a student a question to answer and she will learn the passage she has just read. Teach her how to ask questions, and she will learn how to learn for the rest of her life.
>
> —James R. Gavelek & Taffy E. Raphael (1985, p. 103)

Barak Rosenshine, Carla Meister, and Saul Chapman (1996) reviewed 26 studies for the purposes of evaluating the impact of students' question generation on both reading and listening comprehension—and learning how most effectively to teach this strategy to students. The researchers found that the most powerful way to teach students question generation that improves achievement is to use generic question stems and generic questions. Here are some examples of generic question stems:

- How are . . . and . . . alike?
- What is the main idea of . . .?
- What are the strengths and weaknesses of . . .?
- How does . . . affect . . .?
- How does . . . tie in with what we have learned before?
- How is . . . related to . . .?
- What is a new example of . . .?
- What conclusions can you draw about . . . ?
- Why is it important that . . .? (p. 200)

Here are examples of generic questions:

- How does this passage or chapter relate to what I already know about the topic?
- What is the main idea of this chapter or passage?
- What are the five important ideas that the author develops that relate to the main idea?
- How does the author put the ideas in order?
- What are the key vocabulary words? Do I know what they all mean?
- What special things does the passage make me think about? (p. 200)

The studies that examined use of generic question stems and generic questions included grade levels ranging from sixth through college. Rosenshine, Meister, and Chapman found no studies using these types of prompts in the lower grades (p. 191). This is not to say that younger children cannot be successfully taught generic stems and questions, only that the reviewers found no research focusing on their use.

A strategy frequently used in the lower grades is the provision of question starters—*signal words* such as *who, what, where, when, why,* and *how.* Students can learn to use these words to formulate their questions when teachers provide direct instruction, model their use, afford students time for practice with feedback, and incorporate this strategy as a part of their lesson structure for reading. Rosenshine and colleagues identified seven studies, ranging from Grades 3 to 8, in which this strategy was used successfully (pp. 190-191).

Elements of Effective Instruction in Question Generation

As Rosenshine and associates reviewed the research, looking for how best to teach strategies for question generation, they discovered nine discrete elements used by teachers, in different combinations, to help students generate questions. Most of these elements are associated with good teaching in *any* subject. They remind us that learning how to formulate good questions is a process that occurs over time—one that requires good models, practice, feedback, and tangible tools and supports.

> The classic concept of learning is that it occurs when the teacher asks the questions and the students can answer them, but the reality is that learning does not occur until the learner needs to know and can formulate the question for himself.
> —Morgan & Saxton (1994, p. 75)

1. *Provide procedural prompts specific to the strategy being taught.* The types of prompts provided will vary according to the subject and the strategy being used (e.g., question stems or signal words).

2. *Provide models of appropriate responses.* Teacher modeling of the correct use of question stems or other strategies is critical. Such modeling occurs at three different points in instruction: during initial, direct instruction; while students are practicing; and following student practice sessions. Teachers can model appropriate responses by providing sample questions, using corrective feedback appropriately, and bringing attention to particularly good student questions.

3. *Anticipate potential difficulties.* Teachers often can predict pitfalls for students based upon past teaching experience or their knowledge of a particular student.

4. *Regulate the difficulty of the material.* Students find it easier to formulate questions on shorter passages, so begin practicing with short, simple paragraphs and move to longer passages as students develop skills. Provide stems and prompts during the early stages of practice, but ask students to formulate questions "on their own" (without these scaffolds) as they gain confidence.

5. *Provide a cue card.* Whether you post large cue cards for the class or provide individualized cue cards to students, it is important that students have a tangible prop, particularly in the early stages of learning. Many

teachers we know post the six levels of the Bloom Taxonomy in the classroom—together with key stems—so that students can see them as they ask or answer questions.

6. *Guide student practice.* At least three types of guided practice can help students develop question generation skills over time: teacher-led practice, reciprocal teaching (as discussed above), and practice in small groups with teacher monitoring.

7. *Provide feedback and corrections.* Both the teacher and student peers can provide feedback to students—depending upon the level of learning. Rosenshine cites one study that employed a computer to provide feedback, including an exemplary question, when prompted by the student (p. 206).

8. *Provide and teach a checklist.* It is important to help students understand the qualities of good questions. We can engage students in discussions on this topic and lead them to develop criteria, or we can provide the criteria we believe to be appropriate to the grade level and content area.

9. *Assess student mastery.* We recommend that you develop a timeline for providing initial instruction in question generation. You might plan a two-week unit at the beginning of a school year to engage students daily in learning this metacognitive skill. At the end of the designated time period, it is important to assess student mastery on an individual basis so that you can reteach those students who require additional instruction. Some students will need more practice time than others. (pp. 202-209)

All nine elements of effective instruction in question generation—regardless of grade level or content area—can support various strategies for helping students become better questioners.

Metacognitive Anchoring

Metacognitive anchoring, developed by Frank Lyman, suggests that while students are reading they ask: "How should my mind work?" This strategy takes comprehension to a deeper level. DePinto Piercy (2000) refines this strategy by defining the kinds of questions students should ask themselves as they read:

- What does this remind me of, or how is it similar to something else I know?
- Why did this happen, or what caused this?
- What evidence supports this?
- How valid are these assumptions?
- Is this ethical or right? How should I evaluate this?
- Do I believe what is being said here? Is the writer trying to persuade me?
- What point of view is guiding these statements? (p. 138)

DePinto Piercy recommends that as students pose these questions during reading, they should write in the margins, highlight text, or use Post-it notes to mark passages or make notes. Upon completion of the reading, students can transfer their thoughts to a metacognitive questioning chart, where they record responses in three columns:

- My questions during reading
- Types of thinking I used
- Why I asked this question (p. 141)

Again, teacher modeling is the best method for teaching this strategy. The teacher thinks aloud as she formulates questions. By exposing her thinking to students, she demonstrates the process of good question formulation.

> All our knowledge results from questions, which is another way of saying that question-asking is our most important intellectual tool.
> —Neil Postman (1979, p. 140)

Francis Hunkins' Paradigm for Engaging Students in Question Asking

In *Teaching Thinking Through Effective Questioning*, Francis P. Hunkins (1995) makes a strong case for the relationship between effective questioning, thinking, and achievement. His book is a comprehensive resource on questioning and questioning strategies and how to use them to teach thinking skills and enhance understanding. Hunkins, a longtime student of effective questioning, received inspiration early in his career from a growing body of research indicating "that students attain higher levels of thinking when encouraged to develop skill in asking their own questions and when provided with more opportunities for dialogue with classmates about the questions posed and conclusions derived from information" (1976, p. 3).

Hunkins (1995) offers a holistic, three-stage approach to teaching students how to formulate better questions:

1. *Planning stage*—"the getting-ready-to-question" stage, consisting of activities that enable students to think about a given topic and formulate their own questions about it

2. *Implementation stage*—"the doing stage" during which students use their questions as intended, but monitor, modify, and revise questions as needed to meet their needs

3. *Assessing stage*—"the reflective" stage of the process when students evaluate their questions as to their effectiveness (pp. 231-232)

During the *planning stage,* students can use generic question stems, signal words, or a classification scheme for questions. We know many teachers (Grade 4 and higher) who have successfully taught their students to use the six levels of the Bloom Taxonomy in both "decoding" teacher questions and in formulating their own questions. Another option, one we believe appropriate even for young students, is use of the Three-Story Intellect scheme—*recall*, *use*, and *create*. (These classification schemes are discussed in Chapter 2.)

During the *implementation stage*, students apply what they have learned about question formulation. They might (1) create questions to pose to resource persons who come to speak to the class, (2) analyze textbook questions, or (3) create "research questions" around which to organize a paper or project. In each of these instances, Hunkins suggests collaborative work between and among teacher and students so that students can receive "live" feedback through the process of verbal interactions.

During the *assessment stage*, students reflect critically on the effectiveness of their questions. Did the questions accomplish what the student intended? With more mature students (Grades 6 and higher), you may wish to adapt the Rubric for Formulating and Assessing Quality Questions (see Chapter 2). If you do, we recommend that you first ask students to apply the criteria contained within the rubric (purpose, content focus, cognitive level, wording, and syntax) to teacher questions. As they gain competence in using the rubric, they can apply it to their own and their classmates' questions. You may wish to guide younger students through a process that focuses their attention on the following kinds of assessment criteria: (1) Did my question seem to interest my classmates? If "yes," what did they do to show their interest? If "no," how could I change the question to make it more interesting? (2) Did my classmates seem to understand my question? (3) Did my question cause my classmates to think? How do I know this to be true?

One of the primary values of Hunkins' paradigm is that it encourages students to think more deeply about the quality and impact of their own and others' questions. This process, particularly the assessment phase, also gives students practice in using metacognitive skills.

What Motivates Students to Ask Questions? The Affective Dimension

Students ask academic questions in class for two primary reasons: to get help when they are confused and to get more information when they are curious. Either way, asking a question in class requires confidence, and sometimes courage, to counter what students may perceive as possible "social costs"— teachers thinking they are "dumb" or challenging authority, or peers judging them to be "dumb," "a nerd," or just "kissing up to the teacher." While it is certainly challenging to help students learn the cognitive side of question generation, it is perplexing to know where and how to begin making inroads to change affective behaviors.

What We Know About Student Help–Seeking Behaviors

Why do some students ask questions when confused, while others withdraw and resign themselves to another failure? This question has driven research on the causes and patterns of academic help-seeking. Findings emerged in four key areas:

1. *Relationship between perceived academic competence (as well as actual academic ability) and question asking.* The more academically able or competent students perceive themselves to be, the more likely they are to ask for assistance (Newman, 1990, p. 76). Conversely, students who need help the most seem to be the most reluctant to ask for it. In fact, achievement scores are the best predictor of the likelihood of a students' asking questions: the lower the achievement scores and the greater the student's perceived need of help, the less likely the student is to ask (Newman & Goldin, 1990, p. 93).

2. *Relationship between students' grade level in school and question asking.* Low-achieving students become less likely to seek help and less engaged academically over the course of their school careers (Good, 1981). Research findings suggest that these students' perceptions of the "social costs" of asking questions increases as they move into middle and junior high school. On the other hand, their more successful classmates— for whom the benefits of asking questions outweigh any costs—continue to ask questions when necessary to improve their performance. In fact, high achievers at the high school and college levels ask questions and seek assistance from "knowledgeable others" more often than do their lower-achieving counterparts (Newman & Schwager, 1993, p. 11).

3. *Relationship between student attitudes about the value of asking questions and the asking of questions.* When students like to ask questions and believe that asking questions helps learning, they are more likely to ask questions and seek help (Newman & Schwager, 1993, p. 8).

4. *Relationship between a student's sense of personal relatedness with the teacher and question asking.* At all grade levels, students who feel more connected to their teachers at a personal level are more likely to ask questions (Newman & Schwager, 1993, p. 10).

We can infer from this research a number of strategies teachers can use to counter disturbing trends.

- Create a risk-free environment and emphasize the value of learning from one's mistakes and errors. We can communicate to students that making mistakes is normal.

- Engage students in discussing the following question: *Do the benefits of asking questions outweigh the "costs" to students?*

- Provide specific instruction in how to ask questions.

- Use pair sharing and cooperative groups to encourage students to seek help from peers.

- Structure classrooms to emphasize intrinsic motivation and individual achievement rather than external rewards and competition.

- Attempt to develop warm and caring relationships with all students. (Newman & Schwager, p. 13)

We know it is very easy to make assumptions about students based upon their external behaviors, but we also know that we can assist these unwilling students only when we seek first to understand what motivates them, then to create conditions that will encourage them to open up and participate more fully in our classrooms.

Emotional Engagement and Question-Asking

Research findings on student help-seeking behaviors make it clear that the emotional climate of a classroom has a significant impact on students' willingness to call attention to themselves by asking questions. Norah Morgan and Juliana Saxton (1994) focus on the connections between emotional climate and questioning in their book *Asking Better Questions*. These authors created a six-tiered "Taxonomy of Personal Engagement" to guide teachers in their planning and use of questioning in their classrooms. This taxonomy, which is hierarchical in nature, progresses from the lowest level to higher levels of engagement. The six levels are as follows:

1. *Interest.* Students are paying attention, albeit perhaps in a passive way. They are not sleeping, off-task, or totally ignoring the topic being presented. They may be paying attention for different reasons—because they like the subject, they want to please the teacher, they're willing to give it a try, and so forth.

2. *Engaging.* These students are listening actively (to a presentation, for example) or participating in a discussion; they are completing work as assigned by the teacher; they are cooperating and "on task."

3. *Committing.* Students are "really involved with it" at this level. They are accepting responsibility for learning, may be totally "absorbed" in the content—sometimes finding it hard to move on to something different.

4. *Internalizing.* Crucial to long-term learning, at this level the light bulb is turning on for students; they really "get it." Students may seem excited or perplexed as their concentration is focused; they begin to see the

connections between this new learning and what they already know and understand.

5. *Interpreting.* These students want to talk about what they're learning—they want to hear what others think; they're developing confidence in their own opinions and understandings about the topic—they're rethinking it even as they talk about it, and they are beginning to think about the implications.

6. *Evaluating.* Students, at this level, "own" the knowledge but may need to confirm it by talking about it with people who have not been engaged in learning with them—for example, at home, with peers outside the classroom, or in another classroom. (pp. 19-22)

Taxonomy of Personal Engagement

Morgan and Saxton suggest that teachers ask themselves the following questions as they seek to engage students at each respective level of the taxonomy (pp. 24-25):

1. *Interest:* What questions shall I ask that will attract students' attention?

2. *Engaging:* What questions shall I ask that will draw them into active involvement, where their ideas become an important part of the process?

3. *Committing:* What questions shall I ask that will invite them to take on responsibility for inquiry?

4. *Internalizing:* What questions shall I ask that will create an environment in which they will have opportunities to reflect upon their personal thoughts, feelings, attitudes, points of view, experiences, and values in relation to the material of the lesson?

5. *Interpreting:* What questions shall I ask that will invite them to express their understanding of the relationship between their subjective world, the world of their peers, and the world of the subject matter? What opportunities shall I provide that will enable them to formulate new questions that arise from their new understanding?

6. *Evaluating:* What questions shall I ask that will provide them with opportunities to test their new thinking in different media?

This taxonomy can be used to isolate, better understand, and identify our students' levels of engagement and to think about the type of affective response we are seeking. Further, it suggests that teacher questions have the potential of stimulating student questions. When students become engaged as questioners, they vest themselves in the outcome of class dialogue.

Other Formats Can Provide Students Practice in Questioning

Students need frequent and varied opportunities to practice question generation and questioning skills. The goal, of course, is to help students develop these skills to the level of automaticity so that they use them routinely in classroom and out-of-classroom conversations. However, as with other aspects of improved questioning, teachers need to scaffold students' learning of these new behaviors as a part of ongoing instruction. The formats below are but a sampling of those that can be employed for this purpose.

We do not suggest that you use these formats as ends in and of themselves. Practice in question generation should always be related to the broader purposes of a particular lesson or unit.

Role-play Questioning

This format allows students to explore questioning as a way to solve problems or gather information. Organize students into teams. One member is the recorder and writes all the questions posed on a piece of paper for reflection after the activity.

The teacher poses a potential problem—for example, the small percentage of registered voters who actually vote. Students simulate or role-play the part of investigators, posing questions that would help them better understand and solve the problem. They might begin by formulating the central question to be solved *(What factors discourage citizens from exercising their constitutional right to vote?).* Then they might brainstorm potential contributing factors *(e.g., belief that individual votes don't make a difference, lack of information about the candidates, inconvenient polling hours)* and identify questions designed to uncover basic facts *(e.g., When do polls open and close?).* Students might then speculate on higher-level questions to ask (for example, *comparing U.S. voter turnout to turnout in other democracies or analyzing voters by education, income, and other variables).*

At the end of the activity, teams compare their questions and decide why some would be more helpful than others in uncovering the basic problem.

Press Conference

Teachers often arrange for visits to the classroom by community resource persons such as authors, scientists, engineers, farmers, grocers, and so forth.

These visits can be more productive if students, like reporters preparing for a press conference, generate questions of interest beforehand. The press conference format requires students to brainstorm questions, select priority (or important) questions as a group, then listen during a presentation to retrieve the answers to the questions.

Students can brainstorm potential questions in pairs before the class compiles a "master list." Allow students to prioritize the questions on the list and select a reasonable number that both relate to one another and could be answered during a guest presentation. These questions can be sent to the visitor in advance. During the presentation, each student has a list of the questions, with a place to record answers. As they listen, they can make notes about which questions are addressed and what information is conveyed. They can ask follow-up questions (or pose questions that were not addressed) after the presentation.

Textbook Question Analysis

After students learn about categorizing questions according to a taxonomy, and after they have practice in thinking about the value of questions, they can learn a lot by examining the questions in their textbooks. Ask them to identify the cognitive level of each question, think about the result of answering, and rate the value of such a question. (See sample form, Analysis of Textbook Questions.)

After students have rated the questions, conduct a class discussion on the value of the questions. Each student might then attempt to write questions (based on the topic addressed in the textbook) that are at higher cognitive levels or of greater inherent value.

Question Review

We often hear teachers say, after students have completed a project, "The students didn't know how to come up with a good question that would guide them into a meaningful essay (or project, or research effort)." This is, indeed, a difficult skill. Students have to devise questions that truly capture their interest and seem worth investigating; are related to the field of study in which they have been given an assignment; and will lead them, in a logical way, through a completed study.

Question review is a format in which students learn how to pose quality questions that meet the above criteria. Students help one another create effective research questions through reflection and peer review. The process, which enables them to "try out" their questions before plunging headlong into a major project, includes the following steps.

Analysis of Textbook Questions

Source of questions: _____

Question	Page	Cognitive Level for Response	Consequence of question—What would student learn?	Value of question (1 = not important, 5 = essential information)

General reactions to questions: _____

Step 1. Individual students (or pairs or groups, depending upon the assignment) generate potential questions for a research project, select one question as the focus question for their project, write why it is important, and begin creating a plan or strategy for how they would investigate or study the question.

Step 2. Each student (or group of students) is paired with another. First, one shares his questions with his "peer reflector," giving a bit of the rationale as to why he selected the questions and forecasting the study that might unfold as a result. The listening peer gives two kinds of feedback. First, she gives *warm feedback;* that is, she gives positive reinforcement to those elements of the proposed project that seem likely to yield strong results. ("A student survey on this topic is going to generate student interest in your final report, so you've got a built-in audience.") Second, instead of giving what we usually call negative feedback ("What I didn't like was . . ."), she gives *cool feedback* in the form of questions that help her classmate consider ways to strengthen the project ("Do you plan to do some background research to see if you can compare your findings to national averages?"). Note: It is important to model warm and cool feedback, provide examples of each, and give students practice in generating it. Equally important is teacher monitoring to make sure students are giving serious consideration to the peer review process.

Step 3. The students switch roles. This time, the student who served as peer reviewer shares her questions, rationale, and potential study, receiving warm and cool feedback from her partner.

Step 4. Students write what they learned from their partners. Then they rewrite the focus question and rationale, if necessary.

Steps 2 through 4 could be repeated, pairing students with different partners, especially if this is an assignment with major consequences. Alternately, this process could be used for a whole-class investigation or study as the class decides on major questions on which to focus their efforts, important questions to be answered, and processes for obtaining the requisite information.

Round-Robin Questioning

The purpose of round-robin questioning is to engage all students in formulating, asking, and answering questions. It is a three-step process:

1. Students formulate seven questions for a reading assignment or unit of instruction—six for which they know the answer and one about which they are curious but unsure of an answer. Each of their questions should be important, clearly stated, and focused on the main ideas in the lesson. Students write their questions, as well as the answers for the six that are known.

2. The teacher selects one student to begin questioning. This student selects one of his or her questions (for which the answer is known) and poses the question and selects the respondent, then prompts and probes as necessary, providing appropriate feedback. The teacher encourages students to use effective questioning practices such as calling on a respondent *after* posing the question, using Wait Times 1 and 2, and making certain that all classmates hear a correct and complete response.

3. The student who answers the question becomes the questioner in the next round, and the process continues until all students have posed one question or the allocated time has expired.

4. The teacher then organizes cooperative groups of three to five students and instructs group members to share the questions for which they don't have answers. Group members try to answer the questions as a group and collectively select the one they are most curious about for sharing with the entire class.

The teacher's role is to listen actively, monitoring both the questions and the answers. She intervenes *only* to correct misunderstandings or to perform management functions. When oral questioning ends, the teacher collects all students' papers for review and assessment, considering the use of some for written assessments.

Twenty Questions

This format can be used with a whole class (which we recommend as students are learning the process) or in smaller groups. One student in the group thinks of a person (General Stonewall Jackson), place (Gettysburg, PA), or thing (the debates between Lincoln and Douglas) related to the topic under study. The rest of the group asks questions that will help them identify the chosen person, place, or thing. They are limited to 20 yes-or-no questions (e.g., *Are you thinking of a person?*). At any time during the questioning, the group is allowed to guess the answer (*Is it _____?*). If the guess is incorrect, the group loses one question opportunity. A maximum of three guesses is allowed in one episode.

Students learn, during the play of this game, the difference between "important" questions—which narrow the prospective field—and silly or "wasteful" questions. They also have to consider their wording because if the question has more than one interpretation, they will not learn much from the answer.

Actor, Actor

In groups of four, one student selects a person related in some way to the topic under study (e.g., a historic person, an author, a character in a book they've read, or someone from current events) and reveals the person's name to the others in the group. The other group members then formulate questions to pose to this famous person. The first student pretends to be that person as he responds to the questions in first person (e.g., *I was very comfortable being the king*). This activity helps students select important questions, word them carefully, and practice responding to questions.

Question/Question

Organize students in pairs. Announce a topic for the pairs to talk about. But stipulate that participants may speak to one another only in questions. See how many interchanges they can complete before they forget and make a statement—or simply run out of questions!

Answer/Question

Like contestants on the famous game show *Jeopardy,* students are challenged to come up with the question when the teacher provides the answer. Although we most often see this strategy used to assess knowledge-level questions, the following example from Morgan and Saxton (1994) demonstrates that it can also be used to stimulate higher-level questions.

The following excerpt is from A Bird in the House *by Margaret Laurence. For what question or questions might this be the answer?*

"I went upstairs to my room. Momentarily, I felt a sense of calm, almost of acceptance. Rest beyond the river. I knew now what that meant. It meant Nothing. It meant only silence forever.

Then I lay down on my bed and spent the last of my tears, or what seemed then to be the last. Because, despite what I had said to Noreen, it did matter. It mattered, but there was no help for it." (Laurence, 1978, p. 93)

Some questions that were suggested:

In the story, what evidence is there for Vanessa's lack of faith?
What does Vanessa say about death?
What evidence do we have that there has been at least one other event which has caused her to cry?
Is there a part of the story of Vanessa which parallels your own experience? (p. 122)

Talk Show

A talk show format offers students an opportunity to experience different perspectives regarding the content under study. In pairs, assign students a role-playing challenge. One student in each pair is to play the part of a character from a recently read play or book, and the other is to play the part of a reporter for the Entertainment Channel. The students role-play, one asking interview questions and the other responding "in character." Alternatively, teachers might select a historical figure or someone from current events to be interviewed by Larry King, Oprah Winfrey, David Letterman, or a reporter from the local newspaper.

Summary of Student Question–Generation Formats

When students have opportunities to ask their own questions, they are practicing habits of mind that can help them think, learn, and achieve at higher levels. The student question-generation formats described in this chapter (and summarized on the following page) encourage and support student questioning.

Student Question–Generation Formats

Format	Instructional Purposes
Reciprocal Teaching	Improve comprehension; develop metacognitive skills
Pair Problem Solving	Promote analytical thinking; promote metacognitive awareness
Metacognitive Anchoring	Promote comprehension; build metacognition
Role-play Questioning	Facilitate higher-level thinking; motivate and engage students
Press Conference	Engage students in active listening; stimulate curiosity
Textbook Question Analysis	Review content; promote analysis
Question Review	Promote critical thinking
Round-Robin Questioning	Identify main ideas; promote retention
Twenty Questions	Facilitate retention; practice reasoning and problem solving
Actor, Actor	Promote retention; motivate and engage students
Question/Question	Practice active listening; thinking
Answer/Question	Promote retention; encourage higher level thinking
Talk Show	Use knowledge; promote higher-level thinking

Questions for Reflection

Encouraging Student Questions:
How do I foster student questions?

This tool for self-reflection includes reminders of teacher behaviors that promote student questions.

Questioning Behaviors	Questions for Reflection
Teach students how to generate good questions.	Do I intentionally incorporate activities into my ongoing instruction designed to help students become better generators of questions? • Do I teach students metacognitive strategies? • Do I teach students generic question stems, questions, and/or signal words? • Do I model good question generation for students by "thinking aloud" for them? • Do I provide opportunities for students to practice generating questions with teacher and peer feedback? • Do I use instructional activities (i.e., structures) designed to give students practice in formulating and asking questions?
Encourage students to ask questions when they need help understanding content.	Do I encourage students to seek help with academic work? • Do I create a risk-free environment where "not knowing" and making mistakes are viewed as part of learning? • Do I develop personal relationships with each student and let them know that I am approachable? • Do I help students develop confidence in themselves as learners? • Do I focus on the development of intrinsic motivation? • Do I use cooperative grouping, with heterogeneous membership, and encourage students to seek help from their classmates?
Reflect on related beliefs.	To what extent do you and your students share the following beliefs? • Students will ask questions when confused or curious. • Divergent thinking is important. • Not all questions have one right answer.

References

Anderson, L. W., & Krathwohl, D. R. (Eds.). (2001). *A taxonomy for learning, teaching, and assessing: A revision of Bloom's Taxonomy of Educational Objectives.* New York: Addison Wesley Longman.

Barell, J. (2003). *Developing more curious minds.* Alexandria, VA: Association for Supervision and Curriculum Development.

Bransford, J. D., Brown, A. L., & Cocking, R. R. (Eds.). (2000). *How people learn: Brain, mind, experience, and school.* Washington, DC: National Academy Press.

DePinto Piercy, T. (2000). Enhancing reading comprehension instruction through habits of mind. In A. L. Costa & B. Kallick (Eds.), *Activating and engaging habits of mind* (chapter 12). Alexandria, VA: Association for Supervision and Curriculum Development.

Gavelek, J. R., & Raphael, T. E. (1985). Metacognition, instruction, and the role of questioning activities. In D. L. Forest-Pressley, G. E. Mackinnon, & T. Gary Waller (Eds.), *Metacognition, Cognition and Human Performance* (pp. 103-136). Orlando, FL: Academic Press.

Good, T. L. (1981). Teacher expectations and student perceptions: A decade of research. *Educational Leadership, 38,* 415-423.

Hunkins, F. P. (1976). *Involving students in questioning.* Boston: Allyn & Bacon.

Hunkins, F. P. (1995). *Teaching thinking through effective questioning.* Norwood, MA: Christopher-Gordon.

Kindsvatter, R., Wilen, W., & Ishler, M. (1996). *Dynamics of effective teaching* (3rd ed.). White Plains, NY: Longman Publishers.

Laurence, M. (1994). *A bird in the house.* Chicago: University of Chicago Press.

Morgan, N., & Saxton, J. (1994*). Asking better questions: Models, techniques, and classroom activities for engaging students in learning.* Markham, Ontario: Pembroke Publishers.

National Institute of Child Health and Human Development. (2000). *Report of the National Reading Panel. Teaching children to read: An evidence-based assessment of the scientific research literature on reading and its implications for reading instruction* (NIH Publication No. 00-4769). Washington, DC: U.S. Government Printing Office.

Newman, R. S. (1990). Children's help-seeking in the classroom: The role of motivational factors and attitudes. *Journal of Educational Psychology, 82*(1), 71-80.

Newman, R. S., & Goldin, L. (1990). Children's reluctance to seek help with schoolwork. *Journal of Educational Psychology, 82*(1), 92-100.

Newman, R. S., & Schwager, M. T. (1992). Students' perception of the teacher and classmates in relation to reported help seeking in math class. *The Elementary School Journal, 94*(1) 3-17.

Oakes, J., & Lipton, M. (1999). *Teaching to change the world.* New York: McGraw-Hill College.

Palincsar, A. S., & Brown, A. L. (1984). Reciprocal teaching of comprehension-fostering and monitoring activities. *Cognition and Instruction, 1,* 117-175.

Perkins, D. (1995). *Outsmarting IQ: The emerging science of learnable intelligence.* New York: Free Press.

Perkins, D. (1992). *Smart schools: Better thinking and learning for every child.* New York: Free Press.

Postman, N. (1979). *Teaching as a conserving activity.* New York: Delacorte Press.

Rosenshine, B., Meister, C., & Chapman, S. (1996). Teaching students to generate questions: A review of the intervention studies. *Review of Educational Research, 66*(2), 181-221.

Swicegood, P. R., & Parsons, J. L. (1989). Better questions and answers equal success. *Teaching Exceptional Children,* 4-8.

Wells, G. (2001). The case for dialogic inquiry. In Wells, G. (Ed.), *Action, talk and text: Learning and teaching through inquiry* (pp. 171-194). New York: Teachers College Press.

Whimbey, A., & Lochhead, J. (1982). *Problem solving and comprehension.* Hillsdale, NJ: Lawrence Erlbaum Associates.

Chapter 7:
How Can a Focus on Effective Questioning Transform Schools? Enriching Your School's Professional Learning Community

Focus Questions

How can teachers work together to improve and support one another as effective questioners?

What difference does a schoolwide commitment to the improvement of classroom questioning make for teacher and student performance?

How does a shared commitment to quality questions and effective questioning help build a collaborative work culture across a school?

Remember A. Well-Meaning Teacher from Chapter 1? She, like most of us, has probably heard of most of the strategies mentioned in this book. But, like many of us, she is not using them in her daily practice. Although questioning behaviors seem simple enough, they are not easy to change—or sustain. Research confirms our own observations: Workshops alone rarely affect classroom practice on a long-term basis; follow-up and collegial support are necessary if teachers are to change long-standing habits and practice.

What can we do to create a school full of teachers who are more like A. Thoughtful Teacher? How can we put into place a support system for teachers as they establish new habits and practices? In this chapter, we consider the kinds of structures and staff development that would help "Well-Meaning" transform her classroom into one that is interactive, interesting, and engaging for students—and also help establish a schoolwide culture of high expectations for both students and faculty. Topics discussed include (1) essential components of staff development programs that affect teacher practice—and student behavior—beyond the initial exhilaration of learning new strategies and (2) our beliefs about how questioning can strengthen and invigorate a faculty's efforts to become a community of learners.

Teachers Learning Together in Community: Staff Development That Makes a Difference

We have been training and working with teachers on effective questioning for more than 15 years. During that time, we've learned a great deal about questioning, school culture, and the nature of change. We think you will find some of what we've learned interesting and useful as you continue your journey of professional growth, so, in the spirit of collegiality, we'd like to share the story of our own journey.

Jackie first developed a workshop on effective questioning for the Montgomery (Alabama) Teacher Center in 1985. Beth joined her as a cofacilitator three years later, and we have "teamed" to plan and conduct hundreds of staff development sessions since then. From the beginning, we were confident that we were presenting important, research-based information about best practice that could positively affect teaching and subsequent learning. Our workshop feedback forms confirmed it—teachers found the information about effective questioning relevant and meaningful; they were fully engaged during the workshop; and they left with plans to use the strategies in the classrooms. What more could presenters hope for?

But we knew that it could be more—and better. Our experience as teachers and professional developers, coupled with a review of research on the importance of school culture and peer coaching in supporting and sustaining the learning of teachers, sparked an intense desire to create something that was "more than a workshop."

So, during the course of 1989-1991, we collaborated with a group of Kentucky educators—teachers, principals, and central office staff developers—to design a more complete staff development process to promote effective questioning. After several months of initial work, we formalized our beliefs about staff development into a statement of philosophy (see page 138) that guided our work. Preceding the publication of the National Staff Development Council (NSDC) standards, these statements still remain important. We believe less in "training" than in the facilitation of reflection and

> Questioning is fundamental. There's not a classroom in the world where the teacher isn't asking questions—you really can't teach without it! We assume it doesn't require special training because, since we've been in school and college for 16 years, we think we know how to question. But being an effective questioner is not automatic. Questioning needs to be developed, just like the fundamental skills in sports, yet teachers are rarely given the opportunity or training to develop those skills.
>
> —Bob Iuzzolino, Director of Curriculum Services, Westmoreland Intermediate Service Unit, Pennsylvania

Statement of Philosophy

Adopted by the KASA-AEL Study Group on Effective Questioning, November 1989

Teachers and staff developers should share responsibility for selecting and implementing professional growth and renewal activities that address individual, school, and/or district needs. The roles and responsibilities of staff developers and teacher participants will vary from district to district, school to school, and individual to individual. We believe, however, that effective questioning is an appropriate content area around which to organize a teacher-driven professional development program. We further believe that the following principles constitute sound practice and that they should guide the design and development of the prototype professional development program on effective questioning.

1. Program development should proceed by reference to the needs, preferences, and insights of teachers and staff developers. To this end, a sampling of these potential users should be surveyed/consulted at benchmark points during program design and development.

2. The staff developer should be posited as the program facilitator or guide, not as the primary decision maker or authority.

3. Participation in such a program is best when voluntary.

4. The program should incorporate incentives to get people to participate as well as incentives to sustain involvement and encourage implementation.

5. The content of the program should be rich and deep; the structure should offer teacher participants alternative routes for growth and development.

6. The instructional methodology should be highly participative and interactive in nature and should reflect principles of andragogy (adult learning).

7. The program should be long-term in nature and should incorporate a process for personal growth and development, not a series of workshops that offer "how-to's" or quick fixes.

8. The evaluation component of the program should provide for measures of teacher behavior change in the implementation phase.

9. The program should utilize guided practice, observation, feedback, and peer coaching as appropriate and should offer guidelines and structures to facilitate these processes.

thoughtful discussion. We believe that the content should be related to teacher needs—and that questioning is a basic and appropriate topic for teacher learning and study. We believe that classrooms for teacher learning—like those for students—should be participative and interactive, that teachers should have choice, and that the process of learning should include guided practice and feedback from colleagues.

Certainly, based on what we have learned since these principles were drafted in 1989, we might make some changes. We have learned from research, for example, that there is no clear relationship between voluntarism and teacher growth and learning (principle number three). Although we still think beginning with a core group of volunteers within a school is appropriate, we are more than ever convinced that a schoolwide implementation has many advantages over a volunteers-only approach. We do advocate, however, that teachers be part of the decision-making process when a schoolwide effort of staff development is being selected.

A second change we would make—given the press of accountability in this day and age—is in the criteria for evaluation (principle number eight). Although any kind of outcome-based evaluation of staff development was rare in the early 1990s, if we were doing the study today, we would include *student* learning outcomes. In that the original intent was to impact teacher behavior, our group decided that the best measure of success would be to study that behavior directly.

And study it we did! Having designed a year-long program of professional development, we conducted a field test of our model (Questioning and Under-standing to Improve Learning and Thinking, or QUILT for short) during the 1991-92 school year. The field test involved implementation by 42 urban, rural, and suburban schools from 13 districts and four states. Each of the schools was randomly assigned to one of three "treatment" groups. The first group partici-pated in the full program, including the induction training, follow-up collegiums, and partnering (see pp. 143-144 for a description of these components of the QUILT process). The second group participated only in the three-day induction training, with no follow-up. The third group participated in a three-hour work-shop session—which represents the more traditional staff development offered in many schools.

After one year, the members of the first group—those who had worked with colleagues across the school and across time—understood significantly more about effective questioning and were using effective questioning strategies more often in their classrooms. For example, after participation in the year-long program, these teachers were asking significantly fewer questions, and their questions were at higher cognitive levels significantly more often. More impor-tant, their students' answers were above the level of recall more often, indicating that students were thinking at higher levels in classrooms with fully trained teachers. These results and other anecdotal findings from more than a decade of working with teachers have strengthened our belief that the design of QUILT, which includes a network of colleagues learning together over time, is critically important to improving student learning.

The QUILT development and research project was funded by AEL's Regional Educational Laboratory contract from the U.S. Department of Education and directed by Sandra R. Orletsky, director of the School Governance and Administration Program at AEL. Based on the results of our field test, QUILT was subsequently validated by the federal government's Program Effectiveness Panel and became a part of the National Diffusion Network.

So, what did our program look like "in action?" What follows is a true account of one school's experience in implementing the QUILT program. As you read it, we hope you get a sense of what kind of professional development program we designed, based on research and experience; how it affects individual teacher practices; and how it can affect school culture.

QUILT: One School's Story

During the 1996-1997 school year, teachers at Alexander Elementary School in Jackson, Tennessee, embarked on a new course of professional learning. That learning involved teachers partnering with each other to improve classroom questions and questioning strategies. Partners went into one another's classrooms, observed agreed-upon student and teacher behaviors, and provided feedback to one another following the observations. Partners also met with their colleagues at monthly collegiums where they shared successes and dialogued about problems encountered as they attempted to transform their classrooms into more interactive, inclusive arenas for student learning.

I worked at helping teachers understand that they needed to improve their questioning. To think more about how we ask questions and how we ask children to develop questions. I really got them to buy into questioning as a focus for our work together as a faculty— even before we began the training. Then I gave the faculty a voice. I asked them, "Who would you like to see trained to do this training for us?"

—Dr. Earl Wiman, Principal, Alexander Elementary School

How did this professional learning experience differ from most of the Alexander teachers' past staff development activities? It differed in a number of important ways. First, everyone—both teachers and paraprofessionals from all grades—focused on the same improvement objectives. Second, teachers were leading their own professional growth experience. A team of teachers had attended a summer training-for-trainers institute that provided them with the knowledge and skills to implement this program back home with their colleagues. Third, partners learned from one another through observations and dialogue and with their colleagues during collegiums. Finally, this professional learning experience was not a one-shot workshop; it extended over the course of an entire school year, with follow-up extending well beyond one year.

Another special feature of this professional learning experience was that teachers taught their students new vocabulary and behaviors that were at the heart of the program. Now, Alexander students know that wait time provides the opportunity for thinking about one's own and classmates' answers to questions. They are also aware that attentive listening will enable them to piggyback on a classmate's response and move a discussion to a higher level of thinking. Young students know about Benjamin Bloom's taxonomy and understand what is meant by thinking at higher cognitive levels. In addition to this knowledge, students are learning these norms for classroom interactions: "We learn best when we formulate and answer our own questions" and "When we share talk time, we demonstrate respect and we learn from one another."

Seven years after the initial training, this program is still "alive and well" at Alexander. According to principal Earl Wiman, "Every year since we began with QUILT, we've made sure it was part of new teachers' professional development plans. We use the videotapes from Video Journal (Questioning to Stimulate Learning and Thinking), we still use the QUILT training materials, and we assign every new teacher a mentor—just for QUILT. Their mentor serves as a QUILT partner and observes in their classroom."

The faculty continues to draw on this learning experience to help their students achieve higher levels of thinking. Hether Pflasterer, who teaches special education to second, third, and fourth graders at Alexander, comments, "At our school, since the principal trains our new teachers in effective questioning, everyone is good at expecting higher-level responses from students from Day 1. In every classroom, we have a poster of question words from the Bloom Taxonomy; Mr. Wiman provided those for us." She continues, "You can pick out children who are new to our school—because they aren't used to thinking, especially at higher levels. Our students can really process and use information—and they get the opportunity consistently, from kindergarten on up!"

Across the school, as new programs and staff development opportunities are implemented, teachers make immediate connections with how these "fit together" with effective questioning practices. Fourth-grade teacher Pamela Dunigan reports, "Soar to Success, reciprocal teaching—it all overlaps. We get a 'double dose' because all of these programs have so much of QUILT in them." As teachers continuously strive to help students increase performance on required state tests, they think together about how they can encourage young learners to become more reflective and facile in making connections that lead to higher levels

Figure 7.1

The QUILT Model
for Professional Development

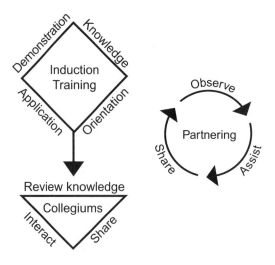

of understanding. *"Just today,"* Pamela reports in 2004, *"in our grade-level group meeting, we reviewed the strategy of round-robin questioning— and shared ways to help students learn how to ask questions."*

Included in the preface of this book is the QUILT model for teacher behaviors, which summarizes teacher behaviors associated with implementation of the process at the classroom level. Figure 7.1, The QUILT Model for Professional Development, illustrates the collegial, schoolwide professional development components that are built into the design of the QUILT process.

Essential Elements of Effective Professional Development

Certainly QUILT is not the only way to introduce teachers to effective questioning strategies, but we believe that some elements of this program are essential for bringing about and maintaining change, as it apparently has happened at Alexander Elementary School. We attribute its success partially to the fact that the design reflects sound principles of professional development. First, the phasing in of learning activities over an entire school year (or two) acknowledges that change is a process that occurs over time. Second, the structure of the program is consistent with the findings of Joyce and Showers (1995) regarding professional learning and change. They hold that teachers learn and improve their performance when provided opportunities to (1) acquire a relevant knowledge base, (2) observe demonstrations of proposed behaviors, (3) practice new behaviors in a safe workshop environment, and (4) use the behaviors in their classrooms and *receive feedback* concerning their performance. QUILT's 18-hour induction training incorporates the first three factors; the collegiums extend them. It is in the partnering experiences that teachers have the opportunity for observations and feedback. Here is a summary of the program's essential elements—elements we believe are vital to any successful staff development program.

1. Modeling of desired teacher behaviors.
During training sessions, facilitators intentionally demonstrate and model a number of quality questioning strategies. For example, they introduce and continually refer to a set of norms, use wait times regularly, engage *all* participants through the use of varied and multiple response formats, encourage true discussion, probe as necessary, and elaborate on participant responses when appropriate. For many teachers, the *experience* of these questioning behaviors is a critically important learning experience. "I have heard about wait time, but I've never *felt* it," said one teacher during induction training. "I can see why it promotes thoughtfulness. In college, my professors *talked* about the importance of wait time—but they never *did* it."

2. Opportunities for practice. Built into the induction training are numerous activities that allow teachers to practice these behaviors with colleagues in a safe environment, giving and receiving feedback. When implemented in a school, the induction training helps to build a sense of community. There is typically much laughter, active engagement, and serious reflection and sharing among colleagues. Teacher response to this interactive form of learning is usually very positive. One foreign-language teacher told us, "I have taught in this school for 25 years, but I've never really talked to anyone in the science department about how they teach. This gave us a great opportunity to share strategies—after all, we're all dealing with the same kids!" Another teacher shared this comment: "[This] has been a highlight of my 17-year teaching career. I see now more than ever that I'm not a teacher alone in the classroom but an integral part of the whole educational system."

3. Formal follow-up activities. Following induction, a school schedules follow-up meetings to support continued learning and to maintain the teachers' focus on the topic of effective questioning. In QUILT, these sessions are called *collegiums.* There are eight collegiums, designed to be conducted over the course of a school year—or two years, depending on the time available for teachers to meet. In some schools, through the use of early dismissal of students or another strategy to allow time for staff development, the entire faculty can come together for collegiums; in other settings, grade-level groups or departments dedicate a monthly meeting to renewing their focus on questioning, conducting collegiums during these scheduled times. These periodic meetings serve several purposes:

QUILT has been a unifying program. Staff and students are looking at a common goal, one we will not reach overnight. Thus, the longevity of the program is its greatest strength. The program allows for individual improvement and does not require everyone to achieve at the same rate. QUILT is a self-pacing, continual improvement program that does not threaten teachers. Each school may write its own plan and gear that plan to its own specific needs.

—Martha Butler,
Elementary School Principal

- To maintain a focus on effective questioning by continuing to revisit it throughout the school year

- To review and "dig deeper" into one specific part of the content of effective questioning

- To share with other teachers how students are responding to these strategies—both celebrating successes and collaborating to address problems that have arisen as teachers introduce and use effective questioning strategies with students

4. Opportunities for observation and feedback. Potentially the most exciting and important part of the design of the QUILT staff development program is the *partnering* experience, which affords each teacher the opportunity to observe and be observed by a peer. During partnering, a teacher models for another teacher her use of wait time, for example. In our experience, the best way to learn these strategies is to "teach" them; and that opportunity comes monthly when your partner comes into your classroom to observe, record, and give you feedback. In the QUILT design, partners observe each other between each collegium, scheduling a time for a feedback conference as well. Ideally, teachers will record themselves, on videotape or audiotape, so that they can also "observe" themselves. Self-observation and reflection are the most powerful learning strategies available to teachers.

Essential Elements for Establishing Enduring Change

Whether you simply want to institute changes in your own questioning practices or initiate a schoolwide effort, we believe it is important to pursue the kind of change that endures. We present for your consideration some essential elements, without which we believe change will not be lasting.

1. Establish clear goals and focus. When you commit to work on improved questioning, don't try to make too many changes at once. Remember that questioning itself involves many different facets of teaching. Select one element on which to focus, and set goals for yourself that are attainable.

2. Allow adequate time. Don't expect to reform your teaching strategies overnight. Let us remind you that while the ideas in this book may sound simple,

We chose QUILT, specifically, because the learning activities and materials provide scaffolding for teachers. They provide careful guidance for teachers, helping them move from acquiring knowledge to being able to apply that knowledge. We also were looking for a program with follow-up; QUILT had it. There's lots of research out there—but very little has been translated into practice and application.

—Stuart Greenberg, Deputy Director, Eastern Regional Reading First Technical Assistance Center; formerly, Director of Curriculum Support, K-12, Broward County (Florida) Public Schools they are not easy. They require a different way of thinking about teaching. Allow at least one or two years to work on questioning as a goal. Mary Budd Rowe (1986) found that teachers could implement wait time, for example, when she explained the benefits to them. But within six weeks, most had reverted to their old habits. We have to admit that Wait Time 2 is still a challenge for us—after 15 years! But we do see the benefits when we are mindful of using it faithfully with a group. These changes require a lot of time—and constant self-monitoring—to make them your own.

There exists within our school cultures a debilitating taboo against practitioners making their work mutually visible. All too often, we don't talk about our practice with others who engage in the same work; we don't observe others who do what we do; we don't ask for help, even when we desperately need it; and we rarely take responsibility for and invest ourselves in the success of our peers. Rather, we occupy what one teacher called "our separate caves."

—Roland S. Barth (p. xiii, in *Peer Coaching for Educators* by Barbara Gottesman)

3. Create a support system. Few of us can accomplish major changes by ourselves. If this is not a whole-school effort, try to recruit some colleagues who will make a commitment to work with you, over time, in supportive ways. You need to celebrate your accomplishments—as well as your challenges. Shirley Horde, a colleague from the Southwest Education Development Laboratory in Texas, encourages us to "celebrate the storms. If nothing chaotic is happening, you can be sure that no one is trying anything new or different." When you set a goal—for example, for every student to contribute at least one idea during a discussion—and you meet it, plan a celebration! Let your students be a part of the celebration. They can actually help you meet your goals!

4. Monitor progress. The partnering aspect of QUILT allows teachers to get feedback from peers. This is especially important because we don't seem to be able to monitor ourselves without a deliberate attempt to do so—and without prompts like a tape recording or a partner. Remember in Chapter 1, the teachers who estimated their own question-asking at a rate of 15 every 30 minutes, when the actual number of questions asked was 50? It's the same for all of us. None of us is very accurate at estimating our own use of questioning behaviors.

But if you commit to a long-term effort on your own, you can self-monitor. Select one behavior on which you want to concentrate. Videotape yourself (or have your students videotape the class while you're teaching). Using one of the sample observation forms on the following pages, code your own questions and, for example, your use of wait time. Ask yourself, "Am I meeting my goal to use wait time after higher-level questions?" If not, ask, "How might my class have been different if I had used Wait Time 2 more consistently?" "What can I do to remind myself to pause?" "How can my students help me in this effort?"

We can't begin to tell you how rare it is to see teachers using Wait Time 2—even teachers who are being intentional about using it! Teachers will proudly bring us a videotape of themselves so that we can "admire" their use of wait time. And as they watch it with us, they smile—not realizing, even as they watch themselves, that there is no silence. So, be aware of possible "gaps" between what you think you are doing and what you are actually doing.

5. Engage your students. The vision for the quality questioning classroom described in Chapter 1 asks students to take on new and different roles from those associated with traditional "school behavior." Teachers must remember that they can't make these changes alone; they must have students working with them in order to accomplish the vision. For example, if a teacher tries to break the habit of calling on volunteers simply by changing the way she selects students to answer questions, the unexplained change can unsettle those students who have a tradition of being "target students"—those who raise their hands, eager to respond. They expect to answer questions. They need to understand the value of hearing from other students. They need to understand the power of wait time, cooperative-learning responses, and the teacher calling on a student without raised hands.

Many teachers have told us stories of sharing with their students that they themselves are learning about questioning in order to engage the students in the change process. Their students think it's pretty "cool" that teachers are learning; many have never thought about teachers as learners and find it interesting. Students can be your best "monitors." They will remind you when you forget to use wait time; they will remind you that an evaluation question requires criteria; they will encourage other students to participate when they haven't answered a question.

6. Reflect on your questioning behaviors. After a given questioning episode, reflect on your own behaviors.

- How did my questions work? Did students seem to understand them? Did they respond at the cognitive level that I intended?

- Were all students engaged? Did all of them formulate a response to most questions?

Wait Times 1 and 2—Observation Form

Teaching Partner: _____ Observing Partner: _____

Date: _____ Time: Start _____ Stop _____

Grade/Class: _____ Episode was: ___recitation ___discussion (check one)

Lesson Topic: _____

Directions: Use this observation form to record teacher questions, student responses, and Wait Times 1 and 2. Write the first few words of a teacher question in the first column. Begin counting after the question is asked. If three seconds pass, circle **Yes**. Record some notes about the student response. When the student stops talking, count again—and circle **Yes** if Wait Time 2 is three seconds or longer. Use the last column to make notes if a student adds to or changes the response.

Question (Write out)	Wait Time 1: At least 3 seconds? (Circle one)	Student Response	Wait Time 2: At least 3 seconds? (Circle one)	Student Adds to or Changes Response?
	Yes No		Yes No	
	Yes No		Yes No	
	Yes No		Yes No	
	Yes No		Yes No	
	Yes No		Yes No	
	Yes No		Yes No	

Prepare the Question—Observation Form

Teaching Partner: _____ Observing Partner: _____

Date: _____ Time: Start _____ Stop _____

Grade/Class: _____ Episode was: ___recitation ___discussion (check one)

Lesson Topic: _____

Directions: Write as much of the question as possible. For each question, circle one word in each of the two columns to indicate (1) the cognitive level of the teacher's question and (2) the cognitive level of the student's response.

Cognitive Level

Recall = Requires recall of facts from memory

Use = Requires using information to understand, apply, or analyze

Create = Requires students to make judgments or create something new

Question (Write out)	Cognitive Level of Teacher Question (Circle one)	Cognitive Level of Student Response (Circle one)
	Recall Use Create	Recall Use Create
	Recall Use Create	Recall Use Create
	Recall Use Create	Recall Use Create
	Recall Use Create	Recall Use Create
	Recall Use Create	Recall Use Create

Teacher Reactions During Discussion—Observation Form

Teaching Partner: _____ Observing Partner: _____

Date: _____ Time: Start _____ Stop _____

Grade/Class: _____ Episode was: ___ recitation ___ discussion (check one)

Lesson Topic: _____

Directions: Record teacher reactions during class discussion; that is, anything the teacher does following the initial posing of a pivotal question. Reactions can take the form of feedback, questions, silence, or statements. Note student response to each teacher reaction. Then check the appropriate column to indicate whether a particular teacher reaction served to sustain or terminate class discussion.

Teacher Reaction	Student Response	Teacher Reaction Served to . . . (Check one column)	
		Sustain	**Terminate**

- Did students seem to be listening to other students' responses? Did they honor Wait Times 1 and 2?

- Did I provide appropriate prompts for students who had difficulty answering?

- Did I give varied and believable feedback?

- Did students ask questions? What could I have done to promote student questions?

Use a prompt or cue (such as the Q-Card on p. 151) to analyze your own questioning behaviors as you watch a video of your class—or as you mentally "replay" the classroom scene in your mind. Carla Breeding, while a middle school teacher at North Oldham Middle School in Kentucky, engaged her students in assessing discussions. She asked them to think with her, for example, about a question such as "What made this discussion work?" and "How was this different from a recitation?"

7. Connect to other initiatives in your work. As you think about questioning, be intentional about connecting it to other programs and initiatives that are being implemented in your school. None of us is very good at juggling too many balls at one time. But questioning is a perfect fit with many of the instructional strategies that you may be trying in your school or district. For example, teachers who have studied Marzano's *Classroom Instruction That Works: Research-Based Strategies for Increasing Student Achievement* will see a natural link to at least five of his nine research-based strategies: (1) identifying similarities and differences; (2) summarizing; (3) reinforcing effort and providing recognition; (4) generating and testing hypotheses; and (5) cues, questions, and advance organizers. In addition, during our training, we usually give examples of two others—nonlinguistic representations and cooperative learning.

We are using Marzano's *Handbook of Classroom Instruction* as a study guide this year. I was just working on the chapter about "testing hypotheses" and "teaching systems thinking." I'm not sure we do this in classrooms. For example, we teach the water cycle but we don't ask, "What would happen if there wasn't condensation?" We teach about the election process, but we don't ask students to think about questions like, "What would happen if Congress selected our President?" Really, if you glance through the Marzano book, many of the chapters have to do with thinking—and these are all related to questioning: problem-solving, the use of graphic organizers, and so forth.

—Dr. Connie Allen, Principal, Natcher Elementary School, Bowling Green, Kentucky

Q-Card
How Did I Do?
Did I . . .
• Plan for this questioning episode?
• Formulate questions?
• Include higher-order questions?
• Rewrite for understandability?
• Plan for equitable distribution of questions?
• Decide on response formats?
• Plan for student accountability?
• Ask the question before naming the respondent?
• Wait three to five seconds after posing questions?
• Hold each student accountable for a full and complete response?
• Rephrase, cue, and clue when needed?
• Wait three to five seconds following a student response?
• Provide appropriate feedback?
• Leave the students with a correct answer?
• Use student responses when appropriate?
• Encourage students to pose questions?

In Chapter 6 we wrote about the connection between questioning and reading comprehension. Clearly, as teachers work to learn how to help students improve their reading comprehension, they will learn about the importance of questioning—by both the teacher and the student. Stuart Greenberg, deputy director for the Eastern Regional Reading First Technical Assistance Center, commented, "Questioning is related to effective reading instruction in two ways, really. Questions are a way for teachers to check on text comprehension—did the students understand what they read? But secondly, as students learn to generate their own questions as they read, this helps them monitor their own comprehension." He continued, "From the feedback we got about the workshop, this was the first time that teachers had ever had the opportunity to think about questioning and develop their skills in this area. For the most part, teachers had been using questions straight from the textbooks. We began to see the discussion level in the classroom moving toward more complex thinking, with students interacting with each other."

Bob Iuzzolino, who provides staff development for teachers in the region served by his Intermediate Service Unit, is informed about many current professional development opportunities. He specifically mentions several connections between effective questioning and other types of staff development initiatives:

• He sees connections between questioning and *scaffolding*. "Right now, one of the key ideas in reading is the concept of scaffolding. If there's one thing we know, it's that questions help you scaffold. Any book that talks about scaffolding in helping learners be better at what they do includes questioning as an important strategy."

- He realizes that questions are critical to teaching for understanding, which is an important notion in the work of Harvard's Project Zero and the work of Grant Wiggins and Jay McTighe as presented in their book, *Understanding by Design.* "They write about the importance of essential questions. How do I, as a teacher, develop essential questions to guide my students' learning and understanding?"
- He says, "Questioning is essential to the *inquiry* method, so important in the fields of math and science, in particular."
- He cites connections to Marzano's *Dimensions of Learning.* "Our teachers talked about persistence and perseverance in order to be effective questioners. This relates to the 'habits of mind' described in the Dimensions of Learning framework."
- He also connects teachers' questioning behaviors to research findings. "Rosenshine developed a framework for instruction and found that high levels of *student-teacher interactions* promote student achievement. This is another reason why questioning is so important."

Questioning as a Tool for Building Community

During the 1990s, the research and literature guiding the design and delivery of professional development mushroomed. Three somewhat independent sources have had an important role in shaping current views about what constitutes effective teacher learning. First, the National Staff Development Council (NSDC) has been a leader in promoting *high standards for professional development.* In 1994, NSDC published its first set of standards (of which there were 27). Revised standards, of which there are 12, were published in 2001. Second, educators' views of effective professional development have been strongly influenced by research about *professional learning communities.* This research relates teacher learning in community to higher levels of student

The turning point for our school came during the initial training. One of the teachers said, "I can't do this in addition to everything else I'm doing." Her colleague (one of the teachers who had attended the training for trainers) responded, 'What we want you to understand is we're not asking you to do anything in addition to what you're already doing. You're already asking questions. This is not new. This is a way for you to sharpen your questioning skills—to become clear, in your own mind, about what you want to know from your students and what you want them to think about and learn.' The trainers were very clear that it wasn't about adding a layer. It was to help teachers sharpen their focus.

—Dr. Earl Wiman, Principal, Alexander Elementary School

achievement (McLaughlin & Talbert, 1993, 2001). Finally, the emergent focus on *learning organizations* in the private sector, which was heralded by the 1990 publication of Peter Senge's *The Fifth Discipline,* has also had a real impact on professional learning in schools.

What role does questioning play in the attainment of a learning community where teachers work together collegially, around a shared goal related to student achievement, and conduct open and honest conversations about effective strategies, knotty problems, and common concerns? Effective questioning, paired with skilled and intentional listening, helps to establish a climate for this kind of interchange. As teachers become more skilled in questioning—and in the equally essential skill of "listening to understand"—they can use these skills to create shared meaning.

Imagine a study group or faculty meeting in which everyone dropped defensive and argumentative postures to pose questions that would help them better understand a colleague's point of view. Before their meeting, they would have collaboratively established norms for their group—norms that encourage listening, taking turns, respecting others' opinions, and using wait times. During such a gathering, you might hear teachers doing the following:

- Rephrasing a colleague's statement to be sure they understand what has been said. For example, "When you say that some of your students 'can't write,' do you mean that they have difficulty organizing their thoughts on paper?"

- Asking questions that elicit more information. "I think it's great that your students write in journals. I'm interested in how you introduced this strategy to them. Can you share what you have done to help them become more reflective?"

- Asking clarifying questions. "When we say that we have a 'discipline problem,' what do we mean? Let's get more specific about that. How many students are referred to the office every day?"

- Checking to be sure that all voices are heard. "Clara, we haven't heard from you. What are you thinking about this issue?"

- Using a system for turn taking—for example, passing a "talking stick" to provide a speaker with uninterrupted airtime.

- Monitoring the use of wait times. "We're getting excited, and I know we have lots of ideas to share. But let's remember to use Wait Time 2 and give people time to finish their thoughts before we 'jump in' with our own ideas."

- Elaborating on others' ideas. "I'd like to piggyback on what Margaret said a while back. If we all agree to focus on math, I could use an activity where we use graphs to study the population growth in the United States."

- Respecting others' points of view—and providing affirmation, even if their views are not in alignment with your own. "I know you feel strongly about our emphasis on state test results. I sometimes get discouraged about that too. But I think the reality is we are accountable for student learning. Could we talk about some other ways that we might assess student learning?"
- Asking questions to get behind one's own thinking. "Let me think about this a minute. I wonder what's behind my reactive stance toward that idea? I'd like to suggest some quiet time for us to do some reflective writing. That might help me know where my reactions are coming from."

A committed listener helps people think more clearly, work through unresolved issues, and discover the solutions they have inside them. This often involves listening beyond what people are saying to the deeply held beliefs and assumptions that are shaping their actions.

—Robert Hargrove (1995, p. 57)

Questions are a powerful tool in helping to build relationships because asking a question encourages us to become better listeners—and more "present" for another person. Listening and questioning to understand are really the only ways we can truly learn about another's point of view. When people are asked a question—and then are genuinely listened to—they feel heard. Stephen R. Covey has called "being heard" the psychological equivalent of air; it is a basic need for all of us. The skill of questioning deepens all communication and interchanges; but most particularly, in work groups, where people are learning together, the skill of questioning takes learners to new heights.

Questioning Is Essential to Student *and* Teacher Learning

A schoolwide commitment to quality questions and questioning strategies affects both adult and student learning. When all teachers in a school focus on the improvement of classroom questioning practices, they and their students benefit in a number of ways. Teachers are able to support one another as they work to change deeply ingrained habits and behaviors. Students do not have to "change gears" as they move from one teacher to another in a school; they know that the norms for questioning and learning will be the same across all classrooms. Additionally, students and teachers are working together to change norms and structures related to such issues as respondent selection and wait times. These changes enhance student learning and achievement.

Improved questions and questioning support continuous school improvement across all program and curricular areas. When adults in schools are more cognizant of effective questioning strategies, their dialogue becomes richer, deeper, and more productive. Continuously improving schools have cultures that reward *asking questions about how we can become even better* as opposed to *always having the "right answers," justifying behaviors, or resting on laurels.*

Most important perhaps, increased attention to questioning and listening improves relationships between adults and between and among students. And, to paraphrase Michael Fullan: All positive change is about improving relationships. The focus on effective questioning enhances both sides of the learning equation—the cognitive and the affective—for both adults and students.

Questions for Reflection

Becoming a Quality Questioner:
Learning in Community

*This tool for self-reflection includes suggestions for creating
a culture of continuous improvement that supports effective questioning.*

Culture for Continuous Improvement	Questions for Reflection
Reflect on questioning practices and strive to improve.	Do I think about questioning and intentionally plan for effective questioning in the classroom? • Do I pose effective questions that are purposeful, focused, clear, and at a specific cognitive level to engage students? • Do I engage all students during questioning episodes and hold them all accountable for responding? • Do I use feedback that extends student thinking? • Do I have a classroom in which students pose questions— of me, of one another, and of themselves?
Students understand quality questions and questioning practices.	Have I included students in my efforts to create a classroom for effective questioning? • Do students understand a cognitive taxonomy and think about the level of the question as they formulate a response at the same level? • Do students understand they are responsible for answering (at least to themselves) all questions posed? • Do students know about and honor wait times? • Do students feel free to pose questions? • Do students talk to and listen to one another? • Do students ask high-quality questions?
Quality questioning is continuously monitored and assessed.	To what extent do I monitor and assess my questioning practices? • Have I established a goal for improvement in my questioning practices? • Do I have at least one colleague who observes me to give me feedback on specific questioning practices? • Do I engage students in reflecting with me on the use of effective questioning in the classroom?
Work with colleagues to practice and improve questioning.	Is there an opportunity for me to work with colleagues to improve our classroom practice? • Does our entire faculty participate together in supporting efforts to improve? • Do we have norms that guide interactions during our meetings? For example, do we ask questions to seek to understand others' points of view? Do we listen with respect? Do we make sure that all voices are heard?

References

Dillon, J. T. (1984). *Teaching and the act of questioning* (Fastback 194). Bloomington, IN: Phi Delta Kappa Educational Foundation.

Gottesman, B. L. (2000). *Peer coaching for educators* (2nd ed.). Lanham, MD: Rowman & Littlefield.

Hargrove, R. (1995). *Masterful coaching: Extraordinary results by impacting people and the way they think and work together.* San Francisco: Jossey-Bass.

Joyce, B., & Showers, B. (1995). *Student achievement through staff development* (2nd ed.). White Plains, NY: Longman Publishers.

Marzano, R. (2001). *Classroom instruction that works: Research-based strategies for increasing student achievement.* Alexandria, VA: Association for Supervision and Curriculum Development.

McLaughlin, M. W., & Talbert, J. E. (1993). *Contexts that matter for teaching and learning.* Stanford, CA: Stanford University, Center for Research on the Contexts of Teaching.

McLaughlin, M. W., & Talbert, J. E. (2001). *Professional communities and the work of high school teaching.* Chicago: University of Chicago Press.

National Staff Development Council. (2001). *NSCD standards for staff development* (revised). Available online at www.nsdc.org/standards/index.cfm.

Rowe, M. (1986, January-February). Wait time: Slowing down may be a way of speeding up. *Journal of Teacher Education,* 43-48.

Senge. P. (1990). *The fifth discipline: The art and practice of the learning organization.* New York: Currency Doubleday.

Walsh, J., & Sattes, B. (2000). *Inside school improvement: Creating high-performing learning communities.* Charleston, WV: AEL.

Wiggins, G., & McTighe, J. (2000). *Understanding by design.* Englewood Cliffs, NY: Prentice-Hall.

Chapter 8:
How Can We Become Better Questioners? Committing to Continuous Professional Development

Focus Questions

What are my strengths in the area of classroom questioning?

What are my priority areas for growth in this area?

What can I expect as I attempt to improve?

How will I respond to challenges along the way?

Changing long-established practice is difficult work, even when we know a new practice will benefit students. Changing classroom questioning practice is particularly challenging, not only because we are usually attempting to break deeply entrenched habits, but also because few of us have had good models to learn from.

When we talk with teachers about why most of our questioning fails to meet the standards of best practice, we hear the same answers—whether we are in New York, Florida, Texas, Tennessee, or Hawaii: "Teachers teach the way they were taught." "Teachers lack the knowledge or skill." "Classrooms are fast paced, and teachers are under pressure to cover curriculum." "Change is difficult." All of these statements are true, at least for many of us.

So, when we hear success stories from teachers who have undertaken our comprehensive process of professional learning about questioning, we are gratified and reinforced in our belief that questioning is a prime area for professional growth for all of us—even for the most effective teachers. One such story came from Jane Hashey of Vestal, New York, five years after she participated in one of our training sessions:

> The overall idea of looking at questioning thoroughly was something I'd never given myself the opportunity to do. I had had lots of the pieces—Bloom Taxonomy, wait time, etc. But this time, all the pieces were put

together; I had never seen that done before. The pieces of presenting the question, getting the best student response, having them ask questions—I knew I needed something like that to bump up my own effectiveness. For me, as a result, I gave much more ownership to my students for their learning. Which made me feel better.

I remember the very first day it "happened" for us in my classroom. I had introduced the norms early in the year and they were in place. But I remember the day when students began to ask each other questions. They took me out of the loop. It happened to be a day that I was being observed. That was terrific, because I looked at my partner and she knew that I had been waiting for this, and we just grinned at one another. It was great to have someone there to share this experience with!

My kids were eighth graders, so they were old enough to handle asking questions. But they resisted it; they didn't seem to want to break out of the traditional ways. I remember it. I even remember the boy who asked the first question. Once that broke through (happened in a different place in each period) my job was to set up the learning, and they ran with it. My classes became much less teacher directed and more teacher facilitated. I did a lot of preparation; but they did the work during class. Which is what it should have been—my work was before class; theirs was during.

We asked Jane: "How long did it take . . . between introducing and encouraging student questions and this actually happening?" She responded:

It probably took about three months. I was steadily using the norms I had learned about. I believe it would have been speeded up if other teachers had been using it at the same time. When other teachers in my school began to use the same norms, the students picked it up quicker. But originally, when they'd come in my classroom, they would encounter norms that were quite different from what they were experiencing elsewhere. I tried to make them very explicit, a real part of the classroom atmosphere. It takes a few months to get that going. . . .

Look at what Jane is saying. Questioning is a process; it includes many interconnected behaviors. Changing these behaviors takes time. All change begins with establishing new norms, and this also takes time. You can't predict how long it will take for students to internalize these new norms; patience is required. However, when students "get it" and become engaged in a proactive manner, it's almost like magic!

Many Discrete Behaviors Contribute to the Transformed Classroom

Questioning is a process; many discrete behaviors contribute to an environment that nurtures *questioning students.* One of the major purposes of this book is to examine all of these behaviors and their relationship to improved student performance. Although most of these behaviors need to be adopted by both students and their teachers in order for the vision to be realized, it is teachers who are in charge of facilitating the change.

And so we invite our readers to reflect on the behaviors associated with questioning and to identify your strengths—or areas in which your current performance matches what research identifies as best practice. We also suggest that you identify priority areas for growth—behaviors you would like to work on with your students or your peers. Later in this chapter, we present a self-assessment for your use in personal reflection and commitment. However, acknowledging that we've "covered" a lot of behaviors, we'll first revisit each behavior and thereby provide you with a quick reference you can look to as you complete the self-assessment.

1. *Revisit your beliefs about questioning and learning.* In Chapter 1 we introduced eight beliefs that we think are critical to questioning for student learning:

   - Good questions help students learn.
   - All students can respond to all questions.
   - All student answers deserve respect.
   - Think time is important.
   - Students will ask questions when confused or curious.
   - All students can think and reason—beyond rote memory.
   - Divergent thinking is important.
   - Not all questions have one right answer.

To what extent do you hold each of these beliefs? Is your behavior consistent with the beliefs? What would it take for you to align your behavior with the beliefs?

2. *Adopt a set of classroom norms that support quality questioning behaviors, and teach these to your students.* We presented six norms in Chapter 1:

   - We all need time to reflect on past experiences if we are to gain new understandings.

- We all need time to think before speaking.
- We all need time to think out loud and complete our thoughts.
- We learn best when we formulate and answer our own questions.
- We learn from one another when we listen with attention and respect.
- When we share talk time, we demonstrate respect, and we learn from one another.

We encourage you to adapt these norms so that they fit you and your students. Some teachers involve their students in formulation of the norms. In any event, it is critical that students "own" the norms, so you must afford them time to discuss them; you must refer to them frequently; and, most important, you must model them.

3. *Carefully formulate quality questions for each class.* Consider the question's purpose, the content focus, and the cognitive level at which you wish to engage student thinking. Take care in wording the question so that it will communicate to your students. Chapter 2 presents a number of taxonomies that can be used in formulating questions.

4. *Think about alternate ways for student answering.* If you are overly dependent upon students volunteering by raising their hands, consider other structures for student answering. Chapter 3 presents a range of diverse response formats, for both recitation and discussion. Incorporate the selection of a response format into your lesson planning.

5. *Involve all students in answering.* Be intentional about breaking up any "action zones" that may exist in your classes. Communicate to your students that you expect each one of them to be on the ready to provide their answer to every question you pose.

6. *Ask your question before calling on any one student to respond.* Address all of your questions to all of your students, making eye contact with all sections of the classroom so that everyone feels included.

7. *Ask your question and stop or pause for at least three to five seconds* (Wait Time 1) *before calling on a student.* Teach your students about the value of using this time for thinking. Let them know that thinking is a process, and that each one of us does this at our own rate.

8. *When students fail to provide a complete and correct answer to your question, use* **cues, clues, and prompts** *to assist them in making connections that will lead to an answer.* Again, let your students know that you will be "sticking with them," that you care that each one comes up with his or her own answer.

9. *Pause for at least three seconds after a student stops speaking in answer to a question before making a follow-up response to the student (e.g., feedback, praise) and before calling on another student (Wait Time 2).* Again, assure that your students understand the reasons for Wait Time 2 and that they have ample opportunity to practice.

10. *When posing a convergent question (a question for which there is a correct response), provide students with appropriate feedback—for example, positive, corrective, or negative feedback.* Leave all students with a correct and complete response to each question.

11. *When facilitating discussion, respond to students in ways that will sustain their thinking—as opposed to terminating it.* In Chapter 5, we presented alternatives to evaluative feedback and shared questions that can be used in the context of discussion.

12. *Prompt students to elaborate on their answers through the use of follow-up questions and comments.* Use probes to encourage students to think more deeply and/or to make new connections.

13. *Teach students how to generate quality questions.* Provide generic question stems and signal words; afford opportunities for practice with feedback. Help students understand the connection between formulating questions and learning. (This was explored in Chapter 6.)

14. *Use questions to help students develop metacognitive skills.* Talk with students about the value of thinking about how we learn and how we question. Help them think of strategies they can use to operate their brains more effectively.

15. *Help students develop confidence in their ability to learn through questioning.* Let them know that when they pose a question they are demonstrating a beginning understanding of the topic. Assure them that asking questions is a smart, not "dumb," thing to do in class.

16. *Help students understand that the benefits of asking questions (i.e., learning and being engaged in school) outweigh the "costs" (teacher and/or classmates' opinions of students who ask questions).* Offer students opportunities to discuss the value of questions and questioning.

17. *Continuously work on a classroom culture that invites student questions and thinking.* Collaborate with students in finding ways to make the class environment more supportive of questioning, thinking, and learning.

18. *Develop an ongoing commitment to improving your classroom questions and questioning processes.* Think about the consequences of believing that one has "arrived" as an effective questioner; that there is no need to continue work in this area. Reflect on the meaning of continuous improvement—the process of always striving to be better, of experimenting with new behaviors and strategies. Consider discussing these concepts with your students.

19. *Collaborate with colleagues in the formulation of quality questions.* Work together in grade level or departmental teams to formulate quality pivotal questions—for units and for individual lessons. Dialogue with colleagues about how the questions worked with kids. Share student responses.

20. *Arrange to observe colleagues during a class when they are intentionally using questioning as a primary instructional method. Invite colleagues to visit your classroom to observe your and your students' questioning. Ask for feedback.* Talk about the value of deprivatizing practice and using a commitment to improved questioning as a springboard for enriching your professional learning community.

21. *Use quality questions and effective questioning strategies in professional dialogue (and in communications with family and friends).* Monitor your use of questioning. Reflect on the impact of your questions. Do they produce the intended results?

22. *Plan time for personal reflection on your growth as a questioner.* Take time out on a regular basis to engage in reflective writing about how questioning is going for your students. You may even want to audiotape or videotape a class every three or four weeks and listen or view in privacy, using one of the observation forms provided in Chapter 7.

These 22 behaviors are interconnected and mutually reinforcing; however, most of us do some of these things very well (they seem to come naturally) while practicing others to a limited degree or not at all. The self-assessment that follows will help you think about the extent to which you now perform each of these behaviors. Which ones do you practice consistently and successfully? These are your s*trengths.* Which ones are you intentionally trying to adopt but still have room for growth? These are a*reas of adequate performance;* that is, you could reach a higher level of mastery. Finally, which of these would you designate as *priority areas for growth?* As you have read and pondered this book, which behaviors really spoke to you as ones that you'd like to work on right away?

Identify Your Personal Strengths and Priorities for Improvement

The self-assessment form on page165 lists the 22 behaviors outlined in this book that can help teachers transform their classrooms. As you rate yourself on each behavior, take time to think. Be honest, but realistic. Be candid, but give yourself credit. Consider this an exercise in reflection.

Build on Your Strengths

As you think about how to enhance your effectiveness in questioning, first consider the strengths that you've identified. Build on these strengths. If you are good at formulating quality questions, use this strength to your advantage by continuing to make your questions even more effective, by calling student attention to the importance of these questions as vehicles for learning, by talking about a particularly powerful question with colleagues, and by offering to share questions with them. Build your reputation as a crafter of quality questions.

Now, let's imagine that you've identified Wait Time 1 and Wait Time 2 as priorities for growth. Think about how your strength as a creator of quality questions can support your efforts to be more diligent in your use of the wait times. We suggest that there's a real connect here and a wonderful support for your intended growth area. Think about it. Quality questions are worth thinking about; they deserve to be put out there and "floated" for a few seconds while students consider them. Quality questions trigger thinking and, given time to really consider such a question, students who have not been engaged beyond the *interest* level may now have an opportunity to move to the *internalization* level of engagement and beyond.

We recommend that you focus your attention on a strength and a priority or two and think about how you can use the strength and priority in tandem (as illustrated above) on your journey of improvement. When we use our strengths as building blocks for our increased effectiveness, we are better able to accentuate positives and release energy needed for the hard work of change.

Real Change Is Difficult: The Key Is to "Just Do It" (Just Begin)

We close with a reflective piece written by Susan Atkins, who was an AP American Government teacher at the time she penned this. Susan, a master teacher, participated in our workshops on questioning several years ago. We believe Susan's piece perfectly captures what we hear from so many who are attempting to reculture their classrooms to make them communities of learners

Self-Assessing for Quality Questioning

Directions: Think about each behavior as you now practice it in your classroom or in another learning environment. Rate your current behavior as a *Strength, Area of Adequate Performance,* or *Priority for Growth.*

Behavior Supporting Quality Questioning	Strength	Area of Adequate Performance	Priority Area for Growth
1. Revisit beliefs about questioning and learning.			
2. Adopt classroom norms.			
3. Formulate quality questions.			
4. Alternate ways for student answering.			
5. Involve all students.			
6. Ask question before calling on student.			
7. Use Wait Time 1.			
8. Use cues, clues, and prompts.			
9. Use Wait Time 2.			
10. Provide appropriate feedback.			
11. Sustain thinking during discussion.			
12. Prompt students to elaborate.			
13. Teach students to generate quality questions.			
14. Teach students metacognitive skills.			
15. Help students develop confidence.			
16. Help students understand benefits of questioning.			
17. Work on classroom culture.			
18. Commit to improving classroom questioning.			
19. Collaborate with colleagues in question formulation.			
20. Observe and be observed.			
21. Use quality questioning in professional dialogue.			
22. Take time for personal reflection.			

dedicated to quality questioning. Susan's message is captured in the title of this section: "Real Change Is Difficult: The Key Is to 'Just Do It' (Just Begin)." We can't say it any better, so we invite you to listen to Susan and follow her advice: Just Do It!

Using effective questioning strategies to improve learning and thinking is an approach supported by research and by many of America's cutting-edge education writers. It makes sense—common sense—an attribute sometimes lacking in programs designed to help teachers improve some aspect of the classroom environment. It makes sense that our students need time to think before they respond, and that less "teacher talk" is likely to produce the desired outcome of more student response. It makes sense that carefully constructed leading questions can only enhance learning.

Then why do I not yet have a classroom where effective questioning is employed every single day? Why do I make temporary progress and then suffer a lapse in consistency, failing to make quality questions a priority for lengthy periods of time? I am reminded of the old Chinese adage, "One step forward, two steps back." Yes, I admit it. I fear I have lost ground since September. I think the answers to these questions are complex, but I believe I have identified some of the factors contributing to my inability to pursue my goals as diligently as I would like.

First of all, I believe that implementing new questioning behaviors on a full-time basis represents a commitment no less complicated than a major lifestyle change. In order to be fully effective and beneficial to the students, I feel that a program of effective questioning must become an integral part of classroom methodology. It should not be just another theory to which you pay occasional homage. Therefore, the decision is similar to genuine resolutions to eat healthier and exercise more. Think about it. You know about the benefits and advantages of regular exercise. You have good intentions. You start out strong. You get sidetracked and miss that first afternoon workout in a month and before you know it, you have fallen back into the "old routine." Similarly, you get sidetracked by all the class time you lost during Homecoming Week, and effective questioning begins to take a backseat to playing catch-up.

Lifestyle or major methodology changes are hard to maintain, whether they involve sit-ups, fat grams, or wait time. Basic human nature then becomes an obstacle to overcome. Another obstacle is what appears to be the worldwide phenomenon of resistance to change. Teachers, like many other people in the real world, are often resistant to change. It can appear to threaten our very kingdoms—our classrooms. It can appear to threaten the academic welfare of our subjects—our students. Some say that this resistance grows from fear. Fear of the unknown, fear of failure, or fear of our own inability to successfully implement a new program or teaching style can subconsciously foil our efforts to commit to significant change in our class-room. Most of us intellectualize that this fear is irrational, but it also is an obstacle to making even a much-desired change such as implementation of effective questioning strategies.

This resistance to change can also be rooted in ego. Most classroom teachers strive to do much more than just a "good job." We want the very best for our students because we respect their potential. We like them. Therefore, it is a bitter pill to swallow that our past performance may have sometimes been lacking and that we really may need to make some major adjustments. It is hard to accept that our brilliant oratory combined with witty remarks and seemingly well-placed questions all woven into a glorious action-packed lesson may have fallen short of the mark. It is difficult to seriously consider that maybe those students out of the T-zone never get enough attention or response time, that nobody got enough thinking time, and that we never once touched those lofty higher planes of Bloom's Tax-onomy.

To admit that we need to change can be threatening. To actually make desired changes takes commitment, consistency, and time. This brings us to another deterrent—the bureaucratic nature of all institutions, including schools. Yes, on the one hand, schools are places of learning. Most seek to create a positive, challenging environment for students. They encourage teachers to investigate new methods, discard ineffective techniques, and incorporate new ones into their routines. On the other hand, schools are institutions with operational concerns such as maintaining physical facilities and meeting financial and legal requirements. As such, schools must pay attention to paperwork, deadlines, and efficiency. The bureaucratic nature of schools can render them resistant to (or literally incapable of) accommodat-ing major change. This can create a conflict.

Teachers who want to more fully utilize the strategies of effective questioning need time—time to organize, time to observe, time to write good questions, time to assess progress, and time to find or develop energizers. Like our students, teachers need time to think. Teachers often feel over-whelmed by the message they receive: "Yes, this seems like a really valuable program that would enhance learning. Go for it! But don't forget that your monthly attendance report is due on Monday, and we must have all pro-posed textbook changes including publisher, edition, and ISBN numbers turned in by Tuesday, as well as proposed departmental budgets. The seminar on computerized grading programs will be Wednesday afternoon, so it won't conflict with the Scholarship Committee meeting on Wednesday morning. Tutorials are scheduled before school on Thursday, and clubs will meet at 12:30 that day. Remember that the counselors need your student recommendation forms and weekly reports and, yes, it's History Week." Examined individually, these and other tasks represent quite reasonable and expected demands from that part of the school that must function as a bureaucratic institution. When viewed cumulatively and added to the responsibilities of teaching and grading, however, very little time is left for the organization of a "lifestyle" caliber change.

Is it possible to separate the school as a bastion of learning from the school as an institution? No. Is it possible to reduce the nonacademic workload of teachers so that they may truly concentrate on innovative programs? Yes and no. Yes, it is possible with additional resources like teacher units and additional staff. No, the funds required to make these changes are not always available, nor are schools always willing to channel those funds to resources that would allow teachers more time during the school day to plan, practice, and implement new strategies.

Clearly, I have little control over some of the obstacles toward accomplishing the goal of using effective questioning strategies consistently. So, what must I do to get back on track? Focus on those things over which I may exert some influence. Set aside ego and fear. Break the overall goal down into manageable increments. Don't let illusions of perfection stand in the way. (No, I probably will never be good enough at using "wait time" to appear as a positive example in a training video, but my students will benefit from my attempts!) We teachers need to listen to the same messages we send our students: Try again. Rethink your plan. Good start! Get organized! I know you can do it.

Questions for Reflection

Committing to Improved Questioning:
How Can I Become a Better Questioner?

This tool for self-reflection reviews teacher behaviors
that can support effective questioning.

Behaviors	Questions for Reflection
Review discrete questioning behaviors.	Do I understand the importance of each of the 22 behaviors associated with improved questioning? • Do I have a mental picture of what this behavior looks and sounds like in a classroom? • What would I need to teach my students about this behavior in order for me to be successful in using it in my classroom? • What are the connections between and among the different behaviors? In what ways are they interconnected?
Identify my personal strengths and priorities for growth in the area of questioning.	Do I periodically assess my own effectiveness in the identified areas? • What are my strengths? • In what areas would I like to focus my improvement efforts? (priority for growth) • How can I build on an identified strength as I seek to grow in one or more areas?
Reflect on related beliefs.	What do I really believe about the following? • Good questions help students learn. • All students can respond to all questions. • All student' answers deserve respect. • Think time is important. • Students will ask questions when confused or curious. • All students can think and reason—beyond rote memory. • Divergent thinking is important. • Not all questions have one right answer.
Just do it!	Am I willing to get started on this journey? • What is my personal vision for questioning and learning for my students? • When and where will I begin this journey? • Am I willing to set aside excuses? • Do I accept that change is a process that occurs over time?

Glossary

action zone. The area in a classroom in which target students sit, **target students** being those who tend to dominate or monopolize class interactions.

affective domain. The sphere of learning that deals with attitudes, values, and beliefs.

clue. A verbal or nonverbal aid to discovering the correct response.

cognitive domain. The sphere of learning that is based upon knowledge or information; the sphere of learning covered by Bloom's Cognitive Taxonomy.

collegium. A 90-minute seminar that (1) encourages colleagues to share their personal experiences in trying out effective questioning behaviors, (2) provides opportunities to review the knowledge base, and (3) allows for the practice of desired behaviors.

convergent question. A question for which there is a correct or acceptable response (other than at the *recall* level of the Bloom Taxonomy). A convergent question requires respondents to narrow or focus their thought processes. It can encompass the revised Bloom Taxonomy's cognitive process dimensions of *understand, apply,* and *analyze.*

covert response. A silent, nonverbal, mental response to a question.

cue. Any verbal or nonverbal expression (usually by the teacher) that assists students in making connections or associations that will facilitate correct responses.

directed question. A question that the teacher poses to a predetermined individual student.

discussion. The form of the question-answer process that takes place when the teacher and students talk back and forth about an issue following an initial question, which is usually posed by the teacher.

divergent question. A question for which there are multiple, alternative, correct responses, not one right answer. A divergent question calls on respondents to open up their thinking. It can include the revised Bloom Taxonomy's cognitive process dimensions of *apply, analyze, evaluate,* and *create.*

educative question. A well-conceived, well-formulated, clearly worded question that promotes a specific pedagogical purpose. An educative question is a product of a teacher's deliberate thinking and composition.

emerging question. A question that grows out of student responses to **pivotal questions.** An emerging question is conceived and formulated during the course of a class by either the teacher or a student.

induction training. The component of staff development that introduces participants to teacher behaviors and the knowledge base on which effective questioning depends.

norms. Stated or unstated group expectations related to individual behavior.

overt response. A spoken, written, or signaled answer to a teacher's question.

partner. A colleague, usually from the same school, who a teacher engages in reciprocal classroom observations and feedback conferences.

perplexity. The state of being in doubt, puzzlement, wonderment, uncertainty, or incomprehension about some matter or issue.

pivotal question. A question that addresses a principal fact or concept in a lesson and is prepared as a part of lesson planning.

probe. A teacher question or comment designed to aid a responding student in making a more complete or correct response.

quality question. A question that focuses attention, stimulates thinking, and results in real learning. A quality question has four characteristics: (1) promotes instructional purposes, (2) focuses on important content, (3) facilitates thinking at a stipulated cognitive level, and (4) communicates clearly.

QUILT staff development process. An opportunity for teachers to pursue a comprehensive and coherent study of classroom questioning. QUILT is the acronym for Questioning and Understanding to Improve Learning and Thinking.

recitation. The form of the question-answer process in which the teacher asks one question after another and students give answers in turn. Typically used to review, drill, and practice.

redirect method. The purposeful directing of a question that has been answered by one student to a different student, usually for the purpose of obtaining an alternative perspective.

success rate. The percentage of correct student responses to questions posed by a teacher in a given period or on a given assignment.

target students. A small percentage of students in a class who tend to dominate or monopolize class interactions. These students are usually involved in three to five times as many classroom interactions as their nontargeted classmates.

undirected question. A question that the teacher beams to a class for the purpose of eliciting a volunteer response.

Wait Time 1. The amount of time that elapses following the asking of a question.

Wait Time 2. The amount of time that elapses between a student's response to a question and a teacher's reaction or comment.

Index

Abramovic, Nancy, 29–30, 81
Academic ability, 123
Accountability, 54, 114, 139, 154; student, 13, 31, 78, 89, 91, 92, 93, 151
Action zones, 60–61, 161; defined, 170
Active listening, 2, 3, 56, 98, 109, 116, 124; teachers', 56, 108, 109, 116
Actor, actor: as format for student question generation, 130, 132
AEL Regional Educational Laboratory, 140
Affective domain, 109, 114, 122–124; defined, 170
Alabama Leadership Academy, 48
Alexander Elementary School (Jackson, Tennessee), 140–142
Allen, Connie, 90–91, 150
Allen, Margaret, 22, 105
Alternate response formats, 61, 64–72; table, 72
Analysis of Textbook Questions, 127–128
Anderson, Lorin W., 31–42
Answering process, 78–79, 80, 86–92. *See also* student answers
Answer/question: as format for student question generation, 130–131, 132
Answers. *See* student answers
Aschner, J. J., 42
Asking Better Questions (Morgan and Saxton), 124
Assessment: formative, 97; of quality questions, 24; of question generation, 120; of student answers, 99. *See also* evaluation
Atkins, Susan, 164, 166–168

Backward design process, 27
Barell, John, 107, 109, 114
Barth, Roland S., 145
Beliefs, 19, 50, 55–57, 73, 93, 111, 133, 160, 169; in Quality Questioning classroom, 8
Bell, John, 48
Berliner, David, 84
Best practice, 15–16, 19, 158, 160; *versus* current practice, 10–11, 13, 17–18
A Bird in the House (Laurence), 131
Bloom's Cognitive Taxonomy, 31
Bloom's Taxonomy, 31–42, 47, 88, 121–122, 141, 158; metacognition in, 115; in question generation, 120
Boys and Girls Learn Differently (Gurian and Henley), 48
Breeding, Carla, 30, 150
Brookfield, Stephen, 106
Brophy, J., 100, 101
Brown, A. L., 116
Butler, Martha, 143

Castleberry, Joette, 76
Central Park East Secondary School, 91
Change, 142, 154, 155, 164–169; current practice and, 12–15; lasting, 144–146; nature of, 137; teacher role in, x, 160
Chapman, Saul, 118–119

Choral responses, 64; table, 72

Christenbury, Leila, 28–29, 58

Classification. *See* taxonomies

Classroom culture, 19, 62, 63, 162

Classroom discourse, 56, 60, 84, 95

Classroom Instruction that Works: Research-Based Strategies for Increasing Student Achievement (Marzano), 150

Classroom transformation, 1–19

Clues, 88–89, 102, 161; defined, 170

Cognitive domain: defined, 170

Cognitive levels, 23, 31, 46, 50, 98, 141, 146; and Bloom's Taxonomy, 41; in Rubric for Formulating and Assessing Quality Questions, 24; student answers and, 15, 47; student thinking and, 7; table, 148; teacher questions and, 12, 15, 47, 83

Cognitive processes, 88, 92; in Bloom's Taxonomy, 32–40; question formulation and, 22

Collaboration, 7, 19, 116, 122; teacher, x, 46, 59, 163. *See also* cooperative learning

Collegiums, 139, 141, 142, 143–144; defined, 170

Collier, James Lincoln and Chris, 30

Communication skills, 56, 113

Community building, 152–154

Community of learners, 1, 6. *See also* professional learning communities

Concept maps, 2, 5

Confidence, 114

Construction questions, 42

Constructivism, 6, 33, 58

Content, 22, 23, 31, 50, 95; accountability for, 114; and Bloom's Taxonomy, 41; frameworks for, 27–30; relevance of, 57–58; in Rubric for Formulating and Assessing Quality Questions, 24; and student questions, 15; and zone of proximal development, 59

Context, 25, 28, 46, 88, 95

Convergent questions, 42, 97, 102, 105, 162; defined, 170

Conversational skills, 106–107

Cooperative learning, 5, 7, 124, 129, 146, 150. *See also* collaboration

Courtesy, 109

Covert responses: defined, 170

Covey, Stephen R., 7, 154

Criteria, 122; for question generation, 120; for staff development evaluation, 139

Cues, 57, 77, 85–88, 102, 116, 119, 150, 161; defined, 170. *See also* prompts

Cultural Literacy (Hirsh), 25

Curiosity, 15, 23, 114

Current practice: *versus* best practice, 10–11, 13, 17–18; and implications for change, 12–15; teacher responses regarding, 17–18

Data on display, 65–67; table, 72

Deck, Anita, 29

Developing More Curious Minds (Barell), 107, 114

Dillon, James T., 23, 56, 77, 104, 108

Dimensions of Learning (Marzano), 152

Dip-sticking, 62

Directed questions, 62, 63; defined, 170

Discussions, 7, 8, 25–26, 49, 63, 71, 95–97, 150, 162; defined, 170; fishbowl, 70–71, 72; response formats for, 65–71, 161; student responses observation form for, 149; teacher feedback in, 104–105, 110; teacher reactions observation form for, 149; teacher support for, 106–107

Divergent questions, 42, 105; defined, 170

Drill and practice, 64, 97

Dunigan, Pamela, 141–142

Eastern Regional Reading First Technical Assistance Center, 23, 151

Educational goals, 45, 103

Educative questions, 23; defined, 170

Elaboration, 103–105, 110

Emerging questions, 49; defined, 171

Emotional engagement, 124–126

Equity issues, 53–54

Essential questions, 152

Evaluation, 95, 110. *See also* assessment

Feedback, 122, 128–129, 150, 161, 162, 163; in discussions, 104–105, 110; in professional development, 139, 142; in question generation, 120; in QUILT, 143, 144, 145; in recitations, 97, 98, 102, 104, 108, 110. *See also* teacher feedback

The Fifth Discipline (Senge), 153

Fishbowl discussion, 70; table, 72

Flavell, John, 114

Follow-up, 95, 110; in QUILT, 143, 144

Follow-up questions, 103–104

Four-corner synectics, 66; in professional learning, 68

Fried, Thomas L., 57–58, 60

Fullan, Michael, 155

Gall, Meredith, 12, 79

Gallagher, M. J., 42

Gallagher and Aschner's Taxonomy, 42

Game of school, 57, 64

Gardner, Howard, 58

Gavelek, James R., 118

Gender: and wording, 48–49

Good, Thomas L., 56

Gordon, William J., 66

Gottesman, Barbara, 145

Grade levels, 123

Greenberg, Stuart, 23, 86, 144, 150

Group activities, 64

Guided practice, 120

Gurian, Michael, 48

Hand raising, 62

Hand signals, 64, 85–86, 108

development, 143, 153; respect and, 109; in teacher self-reflection, 19; wait time and, 84–85
Numbered heads together, 64–65; table, 72

Observation, 163; in QUILT, 144
O'Keefe, Virginia, 95, 110
Orletsky, Sandra R., 140
Ornstein, A. C., 15
The Orphan Train Quartet: A Family Apart (Nixon), 29–30
Outsmarting IQ (Perkins), 115
Overt clues, 87, 88, 89
Overt cues, 77
Overt responses: defined, 171
Overt teaching, 106

Pair problem solving, 116–117, 132
Pair sharing, 124, 128
Palinscar, A. S., 116
Palmer, Parker, 108
Partnering: in QUILT, 139, 140, 142, 144, 145
Partners: defined, 171
Peer Coaching for Educators (Gottesman), 145
Peer review, 128
Peoplegraph, 65; table, 72
Perkins, David, 7, 45–46, 58, 103, 115
Perplexity, 96; defined, 171
Perrone, Vito, 58
Pflasterer, Hether, 141
Piercy, DePinto, 120–121
Piggybacking, 3, 85, 103–105, 110, 141
Pivotal questions, 49, 163; defined, 171
"The Poet at the Breakfast Table," 45
Porath, Julie, 85
Postman, Neil, 15, 121
Praise, 57, 95, 100–101, 111, 161
Preskill, Stephen, 106
Press conference: as format for student question generation, 126–127, 132
Prior learning, 4, 5, 22, 97, 113
Probes, 15, 38, 40, 77, 83, 89–92, 102, 162; defined, 171
Problem solving, 66, 115, 116–117, 132
Professional development, ix–x, 142–152; continuous, 158–169. *See also* staff development
Professional learning, 7, 10, 22, 68, 136–156. *See also* teacher learning
Professional learning communities, 152–153, 163. *See also* community of learners
Project Zero, 45, 59, 152
Prompts, 9, 15, 38, 57, 76–93, 97, 102, 161, 162; procedural, 119; in professional development, 150. *See also* cues
Public speaking skills, 97

Q-Cards, 38, 40, 89, 91, 104, 151

Quality Questioning classroom, 7; table, 8
Quality questions: characteristics of, 22–50; defined, 171
Question effectiveness, 122
Questioning: rates of, 11, 12, 25, 145
Questioning: A Path to Critical Thinking (Christenbury and Kelly), 28–29
Questioning and Understanding to Improve Learning and Thinking. *See* QUILT
Questioning circle, 28–29, 58; examples, 29–30
Question preparation: observation form, 148
Question/question: as format for student question generation, 130, 132
Question review: as format for student question generation, 128–129, 132
Question starters, 118–119
Question stems, 38, 49, 118, 119, 121, 162; examples of, 40, 118
QUILT, ix–x, 99, 139, 140; implementation example, 140–142
QUILT Framework, ix–xi
QUILT Model for Professional Development, 142–150
QUILT staff development process: defined, 171

Raphael, Taffy E., 118
Reading comprehension, 42, 115–116, 117, 118, 120–121, 151
Reading improvement, 23
Reading instruction, 151
Reading Teachers' Taxonomy, 42–43
Recall, 17, 42, 47, 103, 139
Reciprocal teaching, 115–116, 120, 132
Recitation, 7, 8, 12, 25, 49, 61, 62, 63, 82, 95, 96; defined, 171; response formats for, 64, 161; signals during, 102; teacher feedback in, 97–98, 102, 104, 108, 110
Recitation questions, 42
Recitation script, 60
Redfield, Doris L., 12–13
Redirection, 105, 111
Redirect method: defined, 171
Reflection, 144, 163; student, 5, 117
Research: and practice gap, 17–18
Respect, 3, 56, 106, 109, 160
Responses. *See* student responses
Ritchhart, Ron, 59
Role-play questioning: as format for student question generation, 126, 132
Rose, Marie, 43–44
Rosenshine, Barak, 118–119, 120, 152
Round-robin questioning, 142; as format for student question generation, 129–130, 132
Rousseau, E. W., 12–13
Rowe, Mary Budd, 4, 79, 80, 82, 83, 84, 145
Rubric for Assessing Student Answers, 98–99, 101
Rubric for Formulating and Assessing Quality Questions, 23, 122; table, 24

Saxton, Juliana, 15, 119, 124–126, 130–131
Say-it-in-a-word, 71; table, 72
Scaffolding, 92, 116, 151; in discussions, 63, 71; in QUILT, 144; and student behaviors, 5, 19, 126; and student learning, 22–23, 59

Teacher reactions: observation form, 149; to student responses, 96
Teacher responses, 83
Teacher roles, 6–8, 19, 54, 59, 60–64, 129–130
Teacher self-reflection tools, 19, 50, 73, 93, 111, 133, 156, 169
Teacher-student relationships, 123, 124
Teaching model, 6
Teaching Thinking through Effective Questioning (Hunkins), ix, 121
Textbook question analysis: as format for student question generation, 127–128, 132
Think-pair-share, 65; table, 72
Think time, 84, 93, 160. *See also* wait time
Thompson, Charles, 7
Thoughtfulness, 109
Three-Story Intellect Scheme, 45, 121
Tobin, K., 83
Transfer of learning, 26, 36
Twenty questions: as format for student question generation, 130, 132

Understanding by Design (Wiggins and McTighe), 27–28, 152
Undirected questions, 62, 63; defined, 172

Verbal feedback, 97
Verbal interactions, 122
Vygotsky, Lev, 59

Wait time, x, xi, 9, 18, 80–86, 91, 92, 108, 141, 145, 146, 158; class interactions and, 57; defined, 172; in discussions, 104; and elaboration, 103; example of, 102–103; in fishbowl discussion, 70; low achievers and, 56; norms and, 4–5, 154, 161; observation form, 147; posters for, 85; in professional development, 143; in Quality Questioning classroom, 8; research findings on, 14; in teacher self-reflection, 93, 150. *See also* silence
Waldrop, Nell, 92
Walsh and Sattes' Taxonomy, 43–46
Whimbey, Arthur, 117
Wiggins, Grant, 6, 27–28, 152
Wilen, William, 100
Wiman, Earl, 140, 141, 152
Wording, 47–49, 50; and gender, 48–49; in Rubric for Formulating and Assessing Quality Questions, 24
Work samples, 64; table, 72
Workshops, 17, 136, 137, 139

Zeuli, John, 7
Zone of proximal development, 59